DEAR AMERICA

We the P...

...ure domestic Tranquility, prov...

...Posterity, do ordain and ...

...tion. 1. ...
of Representatives.

...ction. 2. The House of Repre...
...in each State shall have the Qualification...
...No Person shall be a Represe...
...and who shall not, when elected, be an...
...Representatives and direct Ta...
...Numbers, which shall be determined ...
...not taxed, three fifths of all other Per...
...and within every subsequent Term...

DEAR AMERICA

Live like it's 9/12

GRAHAM ALLEN

CENTER
STREET®

NEW YORK   NASHVILLE

Center Street
Hachette Book Group
1290 Avenue of the Americas, New York, NY 10104
centerstreet.com
twitter.com/centerstreet

First Edition: August 2021

Center Street is a division of Hachette Book Group, Inc. The Center Street
name and logo are trademarks of Hachette Book Group, Inc.

The publisher is not responsible for websites (or their content) that are
not owned by the publisher.

Interior design by Timothy Shaner, NightandDayDesign.biz

Library of Congress Cataloging-in-Publication Data has been applied for.

ISBNs: 978-1-5460-9167-7 (hardcover), 978-1-5460-9104-2 (ebook)

Printed in the United States of America

LSC-C

Printing 1, 2021

Paw, I wish you were still here to see all of this. I can only hope that you are looking down and are proud of the grandson you chose to raise. If I can become half the man that you were, I will be doing just fine. I love you, Paw. Thank you for believing in me when no one else did. Also, thank you for *choosing* me when you didn't have to!

In loving memory,
Jack Graham Newberry

CONTENTS

Introduction..........................1

Part One — THE FALL

1 Be Careful What You Wish For..........11
2 Fear Is Contagious.....................37
3 We Are the Virus.....................65

Part Two — THE DIVIDE

4 Division Is a Good Thing?..............87
5 The Problem Isn't America, It's You...103

Part Three — THE RUIN

6 All Lives Matter.....................125
7 Fact-Checks Equal Real Power.........151
8 Equality Doesn't Always Equal
   Being Equal.........................179

Part Four — THE RESILIENCE

9 The Pursuit of Happiness..............213
10 Uncensor America.....................235
11 Live Like It's 9/12..................257

Acknowledgments.....................275

DEAR AMERICA

INTRODUCTION

What if I told you a story? Not just any story, but one that would stick with you for the rest of your life. A story that may change everything. Yes, I mean *everything*.

In fact, what if I told you that this particular story would also affect not only your life but your children's lives as well? Perhaps even the lives of your children's children? Be honest; would you read it? Or would that be too much of a risk? Risk, after all, is a part of life, but risks are often things most people are not willing to take. We are driven by fear and the matters of comfort in this day and age, after all.

Yet I wonder if you would be one of the few who would be willing to take the chance of hearing what you need to hear as opposed to what you want to hear. Again, most people enjoy the easy way in life as opposed to what is real—even though what is real gives them the opportunity to grow and be more than they ever imagined. They still choose comfort. It's said that the best stories are the ones written with truth. So as I write, I wonder what kind of story you would like this book to be.

Perhaps you are an action/adventure fan? Maybe a romance novel fanatic? Or perhaps you love a good horror read to keep you on your toes! Either way, what if I told you this book isn't fiction at all? What if this story is full of the real, harsh, ugly truths that we not only need to talk about but *must* face? Most people don't like the truth because most of the time the truth really hurts. So what would you choose? Would you choose to be the better version of yourself and keep reading? Or have you already closed the book and walked away through fear of what's next? Would you choose the truth over comfort, unlike so many others? I guess we are about to find out.

If you're looking for a "feel-good" type of story, this book is the wrong one for you. In fact, what if I told you that if you are easily offended, woke, or simply someone who doesn't like to rock the boat or make waves within your own life, you might just need to put this book down and walk away or just simply burn it, immediately? As always, I am not in the business of telling you what you want to hear; I am in the business of telling you what you need to hear.

The truth!

One truth is that this book is going to be a hard pill to swallow for many people, perhaps you as well. It will. This book is going to make you laugh, cry, and shake in anger, but it will open your eyes as well! To quote my favorite Rocky movie, "The world ain't always sunshine and rainbows, *but*." But life and *America* are *worth it*!

Trust me when I say this: By the end of this book, you will either hate me or love me, but either way, you will be forced to open your eyes to the *real* world around you either way. I love this country and believe I have a calling to make people uncomfortable by hammering home the truth. I do this by relentlessly exposing the growing threat of evil —yes, evil— forces, both from within and outside America, attacking traditional, constitutionalized America. I am a blunt instrument of truth. I have to be. No longer is this just about "run-of-the-mill" political correctness and the usual progressive deceit and lies. It's about stuff for which you might want to cover your ears, or in this case your eyes, but you must pay attention. In this book you will also read about horrors such as Big Tech's usurpation of power and how it is we the people who are the virus; fraudulent fact-checkers billing themselves as media watchdogs; and how Black Lives Matter, with antifa's help, is dividing America through intimidation and race-baiting. That's just scratching the surface of what's in this book. There's mention of a whole lot of bad stuff brought together in this one place, and it's one big red alert! Our entire country is undergoing a real-life version of *Invasion of the Body Snatchers*, and it's not an alien invasion. Society isn't the only thing changing here; the people are. And a war is on the horizon.

I'm also talking about truly sinister forces hard at work to cancel our culture, rewrite the U.S. Constitution, turn high school and college compasses into socialist think tanks, and infiltrate all forms and levels of media and governance. I explain how they are trying to tear down and rebuild our country into a counterfeit America, and they won't stop. So, yes, be very afraid. Dissenting voices such as mine are dwindling in number, headed toward extinction in a world where many American patriots are being cowered into corners and told to shut up and remain silent. Not me. I'm sticking it out. That's why I'm here.

Many of you know who I am and are familiar with my first book, America 3:16, which came out in early 2020. Here, in this book, I take a somewhat different tact, almost entirely secular in how I illustrate what's happening in this country. My goal is to inform and inspire, and to call out by name the detrimental forces coming against us. I want to equip you to be able to handle all this without running away in fear from it. Stand up and do what is right, and stick to your guns, in more ways than one. Be full of discernment. Be cognizant of what's going on around you and grasp its meaning. Know the good guys and gals from the bad. Know what you stand for.

In case you are just now getting to know me and listen to my podcasts, I'm a guy in my mid-thirties and an Army veteran who five years ago was a nobody. I was outspoken but not a public voice capable of delivering my message of love of God and country to millions. I am now able to do so, even though my shtick is a bit rough around the edges; I'm not a "smoothie." But I am honest and I stay informed. Just so you know, this gig wasn't handed to me on a platter; I had to earn it through trial and error, and the investment of immeasurable gallons of sweat equity as well as some risk-taking and prayer. I know there are probably thousands like me itching for the opportunity to speak his or her mind and make a positive difference in this world. Go for it, but you have to work for it.

I come from a broken family, eventually raised by my grandparents, and I'm a pretty serious dude. I don't joke around (much) and I talk fast—not a common trait among us southern boys (I'm a native Mississippian). But there's so much bubbling up inside of me that I need to get out and off my chest, and God has blessed me with the voice, forums, and means to do it. So here I am; take me or leave me, but just *believe* me if nothing else. I am committed to truth, and I detest liars. Plenty of them out there. I am also an avid entrepreneur as the owner or co-owner of several businesses, including the podcast that remains one of the fastest-growing podcasts in the country. Combined, my platforms have reached billions. But I can't do this alone. Thank you for being a supporter, and if you are not one yet, I hope you will come aboard and join me in fighting for our great country.

In reading this book you will be forced to ask the hard questions, the ones that so many people do not want you to even consider to be possibilities, the ones that in some people's eyes make you the enemy. The ones that make you not sheep that simply do what they are told. Yes, the real questions. The ones that hurt. The ones that make you lose friends and family. The ones that define who you really are!

You see, so many people simply just go along with the flow, but I am afraid the time for this has passed. The time to sit idly by has long since gone, and it is our time now to stand up for what we *really believe and what we really feel*! It is no longer time to hide behind a phone or computer screen, afraid to speak up because of what someone on the other side of that phone or computer or screen might say. I know you see it, I know you hear it, and I know that you feel it. Something has changed. Something has happened in our country.

If you are still reading this book, you know the harder and darker truth is that something is wrong with our country. We have lost the thing that makes us who we are: Americans. We have become someone else. We have become something else. However, all is not lost, and we can get it back. The fight is *not over*, this I can promise you!

If you make it to the end of this book, I guarantee you this: The words "Don't tread on me" will course through your veins, and new phrases like "Make *Us*" us!" will be your battle cry!

America is never gone. It is also never out of the fight as long as God-fearing patriots are willing to make the choice and fight for her! So that is what I am offering you: a choice. I have done it before, and I am doing it again because without free will of choice and thought, the whole point is moot. I am offering you the choice to walk away. The choice to simply keep on living your life like nothing is broken and nothing is wrong. The choice to keep on keeping your head down and simply minding your own business. After all, that is what has gotten us to this point in the first place. I am giving you the chance to choose. The *real* question is: What will you do with it?

Are you still here?

Good!

Then let's get started!

Part One

THE FALL

One

BE CAREFUL WHAT YOU WISH FOR

This isn't a book for the weary; this is a book for the truly brave.

There is a dark storm cloud hovering over America, and it's an ominous one. You won't see it if you look out the window, but trust me, it's there. Much as stories of the boogeyman scared you as a child, this threat is far more real. If you aren't scared of it, you should be.

You can feel it in your gut. It's a cloud of discomfort, a fog, a shroud that covers the entire United States, stretching from sea to shining sea and blanketing Hawaii and Alaska as well. The cloud represents the sick feeling in our gut. This is no alien invasion, nor is it some weird weather anomaly. It's a man-made feeling that something reprehensible is happening that we are all part of and have contributed to. I describe it as a blanket of concern that many Americans sense and feel but can't put a finger on or describe. As I said before, you know it and I know it. Something is wrong within our country, changing us—at least those of us who are vertical and breathing—and eventually there might be no turning back. It's the rise of socialism and the stink of liberalism coupled with a growing loss of patriotism and freedoms that are supposed to be guaranteed by the Constitution. Furthermore, it's a growing sense of doom that goes beyond division as it slowly creeps toward irrevocable change. Our culture, our freedoms, our Constitution, and what we consider to be patriotic and traditional values are being destroyed and replaced with a counterfeit "America." Stick with me on this as we navigate our way through the minefield under overcast skies even when there's not a cloud in the sky. This isn't a book for the weary; this is a book for the truly brave.

Those of you who have followed me for years and have read my first book know who I am and what makes me tick—*and* you know what sets me off. What makes me livid at this particular point in time is what has happened to America, what is happening to America, and what is likely to happen to America in these next few years. I'm not going to sit here and blame it on Joe Biden or whoever else ends up as our commander in chief should Uncle Joe not make it to the finish line of a first term. Donald Trump certainly doesn't deserve any blame, either. This stuff has been brewing for years, maybe even a decade or so. Now, I'm not saying we're doomed, but we'll get back to all that.

I'm like the legendary sportscaster Howard Cosell or a plateful of spinach—if you know who I am, you know me because of one of two things: either hate me or love me. I assume that if you are reading this, you belong to the latter group! If you're stuck in the middle, you haven't been paying attention. It's time to wake up. If you detest me, you probably crave any chance to listen to me or read my books so you can find new ways to hate me. Be secure in the knowledge, though, that I appreciate your patronage. With every hateful comment on and death threat to me and my family, you only fuel my passion for speaking the truth. Many people say they believe things, but very few will ever take the backlash that comes with speaking what they believe. In reading this, you likely sense the things I sense. You notice that what is happening in America—producing that invisible yet detectable dark cloud hovering over our nation—involves more than just politics and political divisiveness. There is so much more to all this than what the talking heads on the Internet or TV can get to—or even *want* to get to—in a single day. The darker truth is even if they wanted to talk about the changing of America as I describe it, they probably couldn't because of the threats of "cancel culture" or fears of not being "politically correct."

Something has changed fundamentally within our society, and it's because of what we've *wished for* as a society. We've wished for mass prosperity and great blessings from God, the government, or whatever it is you believe in these days. We believe that because we are Americans, we are entitled to almost anything imaginable as long as it doesn't cost us our free time to be keyboard warriors. This goes way beyond the rights and freedoms guaranteed in the Constitution. I look at where we are as a society here in 2021 and

I think, *Good Lord, you want to talk about our being divided and the world is literally on fire.* You see all this and think to yourself, *How did we get here?* The answer is easy: We got here because we asked for it! We got here because we caused it! We got here because we let it happen!

Be careful what you wish for.

For those who don't know or didn't read my first book, let me catch you up. I was born in the most rural town you can imagine: Caledonia, Mississippi. To this day, the town has only about eleven hundred people in it. It's not exactly a breeding ground for future great Americans that people will write about or at least anyone worthy of getting his own Wikipedia page. Caledonia does have a mayor, but it's very much a part-time position. The town might call up the mayor from time to time to cut the ribbon at a new gas station opening in town or perhaps even cut someone's grass—if you ask nicely, have a can of gas on hand, and fix up some ice-cold lemonade to quench his thirst.

About the time I was getting ready to write this book, I ran into a friend who had read my first book, *America 3:16*. This is a guy who has known me for years. Here's what he said to me after he had read that book, in which I talked extensively about my background and hellish upbringing (at least the really early years): "You had every opportunity to fail. Everything about your story, coming from a broken home, coming from a broken religion cycle, where religion was used as punishment instead of love, where God was a God of being a bully instead of an embracer of those who are imperfect." Even my business manager today, who is a black man, said, "If you take everything about you, where you come from, your education levels, what you've been through, and you put me, where I come from, my education levels, and what I've been through, and you just take the name and the race off of each of us, you will think that I, because of stereotypes in America, was the white male and you the African American."

In case you are really curious, I am a high school graduate. No college. I come from a broken home. I come from a mixed and distorted view of what religion was and what a relationship with God was, and I rebelled against all that. I fought against that into my thirties, trying to figure out what it meant to be a Christian and what it meant to truly be loved by someone unconditionally.

In my youngest years I grew up in a dysfunctional household. That was before I was taken out of my home and my grandparents finished the job of raising me. I joke about it now, that being raised by my grandparents was like living in the 1930s. Even though I wrote about my grandfather, Jack Graham Newberry, in my first book, he has since passed away without ever getting the chance to read it. Let me tell each and every one of you this: Tell them! Whoever those people are in your life, tell them every chance you get how you really feel. Do not be like me and put it into a book, and they never have a chance to read what you *really* think as an adult. How you realize that they saved you by choosing you when you needed to be chosen. Love is great, but love is a feeling. Choosing is something that truly stands the test of time. So don't be like me and put this book down right now. Tell them! This book will be here when you get back.

Anyway, let's carry on. This is my chance to acknowledge him again and tell you how much I love him and pay tribute to him. He didn't get to see just how much of a central figure he was in my life as I was growing up. Because of him, I was brought up with core values, and that was how I became conservative. He is the reason you are all here. If he and my grandmother hadn't chosen me when life wanted to throw me away, I probably would not be here today. That's how I formulated the views and morals that I hold, and why I can now see the world as we know it in America, and it is not pretty. I turned thirty-four this week (early 2021), and over the last thirty-four years I have witnessed, especially in the last ten to twelve years, the deterioration of our society.

I ask again: How did we get here? We got here because we asked for it. Let me jump on that line of thinking for a bit and give you my "forensic" analysis of what has happened in America over the last fifty or sixty years and *why* I believe it has happened. Where were we then, and where are we now?

I started doing some research and thinking through some things on my own, passing it through the "Graham Allen" filter. That prompted me to ask the crew on *Dear America*, my podcast, the same question.

"Hey," I asked. "Fifty or sixty years ago, what do you think were the most important things to most Americans—what did they think about as the most significant factors in their lives?" We came up with five things instantly: (1) faith, (2) family, (3) freedom, (4) community, (5) less government/ more guns. Don't believe me? Think about World War II. You had boys—children—lying about their age to enlist, knowing they had a good chance of dying. Their main motivation to join the military—their incentive to join—was to fight for their country. That's it! The money was garbage. There was no free college. There weren't even store discounts for the rest of their lives for being a veteran. They just believed in America! Though patriotism and sense of duty remain among the several popular reasons young men and woman opt to serve in the armed forces, a RAND Corporation limited survey referenced by *Task & Purpose* in 2018 showed that more than half serve because of what awaits them when they get out. It's a 180-degree turn: "What's in it for economic purposes, such as the need for a job or because of the financial benefits such as health care, active-duty tuition assistance, and post-me? To heck with my service support structures like the GI Bill. Times have changed." It's not patriotism, and it's not just about patriotism and serving one's country. Now it's "If you do this for six or however many years, you get to go to college and have it paid for." It's a form of bribery. I realize that this motivation doesn't apply to everyone who joins today, but many of my fellow veterans and families of veterans out there know what I'm saying.

The men and women who came of age during the 1940s were called the Greatest Generation. They saw, felt, and understood what we're now feeling in 2021: that something was wrong with the world. In their case it was Adolf Hitler and Nazism. Now, *that* was a true world threat. Compared to that, covid-19—and the debates about whether you should wear one mask or two in public—is nothing. What there was in World War II was big enough that young men felt compelled to lie about how old they were so they could get on a boat, storm the beaches of Normandy, and in so doing most likely die.

Back then, we fundamentally believed in something much bigger than ourselves. This was around a time when America still believed in the fundamental principal of *E pluribus unum*—"Out of many, one." I mean, why should that be so difficult to grasp? Why are some people now determined to flush American ideals down the toilet? For example, various groups of people have long been calling for the removal of all references to "God" from US currency and other federal- and state-authorized currencies. Or the recent trend of some athletes, starting with former National Football League player Colin Kaepernick, to shun the American flag during the playing of the national anthem before games. There have even been reports of a movement to consider a second national anthem in recognition of African Americans, with the song "Lift Every Voice and Sing" mentioned as one possibility (and discussed in more detail later in this book). No matter how you slice it, each of those cases involves a splintering among Americans in terms of their regard for long-held national icons. "Out of many, one" refers to thirteen states coming together as one nation; the way I see it, those three examples pull in the opposite direction. What do they gain by this apparent rejection or at least indifference to such idealistic icons? What does America gain by it?

One of the key things in America is that millions of people of all different races, backgrounds, religions, sexual preferences, and political preferences should be able to agree that we are Americans, even though we are not all the same. We are all very different, but even with that reality of diversity, we still choose to live here, and we choose to claim this land as ours. This is a selfless mentality that survived through to at least the 1960s, but what has happened since then? What happened to change our core values?

Let's go back to that idea of the five things that were most important to Americans fifty-plus years ago. As noted earlier, they were faith, family, freedom, community, and the right to bear arms. There's nothing complicated there; it's not hard to figure those out if you were alive then. So, what are the top five things now? It's a different story. If you had to list the top five things most people care about in 2021, what would they be? After much debate, because they were much harder to identify, we came up with these: (1) Themselves. Looking out for No. 1 ahead of neighbors (assuming you even know your neighbors). (2) Free money from the government (the list of handouts keeps getting longer, with pandemic-related tax-free stimulus checks being the latest craze). (3) Free medical care. The idea of universal health care, much of it to be available at no cost, gained steam during the 2020 Democratic campaign for president, thanks mainly to the influence of candidate and avowed socialist Bernie Sanders. (4) Your truth, not *the* truth. One person's opinion, even if half-cocked, is required to be another person's truth, much like opposite sides of the covid-19 debate (masks versus no masks, etc.), each claiming science was on *their* side only. (5) Student debts. Anyone burdened by student debt should be a victim, right? It's not their fault that they went to a school knowing they didn't have a snowball's chance in Hades of affording its cost (again, free money all around). When did the US government become a humongous cash cow, with an ATM located in every home across America? "America, home of the free" has a whole new meaning.

Faith is nonexistent, at least in terms of being on the present-day list of five. Expand that list to ten or fifteen things, and chances are that faith still won't make the cut. "In God we trust"? Not so much. Think about it; the talk gets louder each year about taking that motto off the US currency. Trust in God for what? Duhhh. And forget the family. Nobody gives a crap about the family, at least not as an institution. Be honest: How many of you care more about how many followers and likes you have on Facebook and/or if somebody else is taking care of you? Easy Street. And you still call yourself an American?

So how did we get from "faith, family, and freedom" to "me, myself, and I" within the space of sixty or seventy years? You think that that's a long time and that, of course, beliefs can change drastically over such a span of time? Ask people sixty or seventy years old how fast their life has gone by, and they will tell you that it's happened so quickly. It's a blink of an eye when you place that passage of time next to the history of the world, and the change from "faith, family, and freedom" to "me, myself, and I" has happened in record time!"

I believe it takes three to four decades or three to four generations to feel the pain or repercussions of the sins that came before. In the 1960s a selfish movement came in. The free-love thing started happening. In the sixties, the concept of a traditional nuclear family started being attacked. A big part of that was influenced by Hollywood, with movies such as *A Guide to the Married Man* and *Bob & Carol & Ted & Alice* titillating millions of viewers with suggestive depictions of extramarital affairs and broken marriages. That had been preceded a decade earlier, in the fifties, by the start of the communal family breakdown. All that part of a post–World War II society that ditched a commitment to sacrifice and earning your way and subbed in entitlement and enablement. It caused the softening of America, now quickly becoming a nation of convenience, and what's in it for me? Again, be careful what you wish for.

TV dinners and electronic garage doors ruined America. This started happening in the fifties, with the likes of Quaker Foods and Swanson's commanding the biggest shares of the frozen-meal market starting around 1954. Before massive television sets came along and started populating households (eventually with multiple sets occupying most homes), every night was family dinner or supper time. The only thing people had to do was eat, sit around the table, converse among themselves about their problems, what happened at work, what happened at school, what they were going to do on the weekend. There were no distractions. It was a communal family thing that put the emphasis on family. Children knew that, and they stuck to it. After school and before dinner, they would go outside and play with other kids in the neighborhood. They bided by the parental instruction that they were to come home when the streetlights came on, meaning that there was no longer enough light to play. Besides, dinner was ready. No ifs, ands, or buts. You had to wash your hands before dinner; you had to sit at the table properly (keep your elbows off the table); and you did not touch your food before your mother did out of deference to her—after all, she had prepared and cooked the meal! And *no one* touched his or her food until grace was said and the food blessed.

Then came TV dinners, which ruined the integrity of the communal family. A TV dinner is super simple: you cook it in five minutes, it's done. This is consistent with the emerging selfish mentality that says, *I'm tired of cooking for an hour for these ungrateful kids. I'm just going to pop this in the oven for five minutes, then we're going to eat.* Now you're no longer part of a communal family. You're focused on what's coming out of the television; it's your new master. You eat. You do not speak. You do not do anything. The TV is programming you, telling you what you should think, feel, listen to, and experience and where you should want to go to.

Likewise, garages with electric door openers inflict their damage on a sense of community, one in which most women stayed home all day while the men went to their jobs. A job was nine to five, which required the men to leave their homes at the same time in the morning, then come home at the end of the day at pretty much the same time. Because no one had easy-in, easy-out garages, they parked in their driveways or on the street, where everyone could see everyone else, wait for and yell to everyone coming and going, and even chat with one another for a brief period. They might also grab the newspaper or get the mail out of the mailbox, naturally reacting with the community members around them. Electronic garage door openers were a curiosity at first, installed and enjoyed by a small cluster of homeowners but eventually the world. Then the enclosed garage became standard, and everybody had to have one. Neighbors were still neighbors but no longer conducted friendly interactions with one another. Instead, at day's end you turned into the driveway, opened the garage door, drove your car in, and closed the door behind you. Good-bye, world. These days, because of covid-19, the Uber Eats guy drops off the takeout meal you ordered at the front door. You never even have to speak to anyone. You grab your food, you sit on the couch, and, boom, you go right in front of the TV. I will say it again: TV dinners and garages started the ruin of America.

In the 1960s, the nuclear family came under even more attack. Chalk it up to the free-love movement: "Why do we have to be married and committed to only one person? We're animals with animal instincts, it's not natural to be celibate before marriage. Nor is it natural to be monogamous. What's natural is for us to bang whomever we want to bang at any time." That led to a recalibration of our moral compass—in effect, a 180-degree turn. What had once been wrong was now right. Wrong is right; right is wrong. A guiding light was replaced by darkness as many turned from being selfless to being selfish. It's difficult to be married and even more difficult *not* to have sex with anyone and everyone you want to. Let's be honest here: even those who love their spouses are tempted on a daily basis. Science also now tells us that we have chemical reactions going on inside us that trigger animalistic, free-love longings. How convenient; we now find physiological justification for our actions, so how can we be expected to control them? It's not our fault, and it sure is fun and pleasurable. We were once taught to have self-control; now the green light stays on all the time.

Each subsequent decade has brought a new breakdown of barriers that at one time had been unassailable. In the 1970s, we threw off even more inhibitions. Alcohol and drug use became widespread and more out in the open as people exercised their free will to do whatever they wanted whenever they wanted and wherever they desired. Today, the desire to experience bliss overrides good sense. In the 1980s, it was the rise of the MTV Generation with mass distribution of programming via satellite and cable and a TV in every room. That marked the *real* revolution of television, accompanied by the explosion of movie theaters and multiplexes throughout America. Music videos are now reprogramming us, as is cable television in general. Both tell us that we should be able to do whatever we want, have all the money we've ever wanted to have, drink booze and do drugs and have sex with whomever we want to, and it doesn't matter what happens.

Fast-forward to the 1990s, which gave us the advent of the Internet Age and, in 1996, passage of Section 230 of the Communications Decency Act as well as, in 1998, Section 512 of the Digital Millennium Copyright Act. As described on the Internet Association website (http://internetassociation. org), these laws "enable the modern Internet to function by allowing everyone to post content online, and by providing intermediary liability protections to websites and apps to allow them to remove or moderate inappropriate content."

Such content moderation might have sounded reasonable and been considered forward thinking at the time. Nearly twenty-five years later, though, the laws have been rolled out in defense of "Big Tech" companies such as Facebook and Twitter, which have exercised almost godlike powers in determining what posted content is appropriate and which isn't. In so doing, they essentially censored the free speech of a sitting US president, Donald Trump, deleting his posts on the likes of Facebook and Twitter and blocking his access to them. Big Tech claimed that its squelching of Trump's free speech was justified by his alleged incitement of the riots at the US Capitol building in January 2021, a charge vehemently denied by Trump's defense lawyers during Trump's second impeachment hearings and trial.

In early May 2021, Facebook's oversight board ruled that Trump's Facebook ban, which was meted out after the Capitol riots in January 2021, would remain in effect, while stipulating that it would be up to Facebook itself to make a final ruling by November 2021 as to whether the ban would become permanent. In rendering its decision, the oversight board said that Facebook's decision to ban Trump (Twitter did the same, by the way) was "indeterminate and baseless," adding that whatever standards it applied to Trump in banning him should be "consistent with the rules that are applied to other users of its platform." Speaking at a press conference, oversight board cochair Helle Thorning-Schmidt said, "We are telling Facebook to go back and be more transparent about how it assesses these things. Treat all users the same and don't give arbitrary penalties."

In responding to the board's decision, Facebook said it would "consider the board's decision and determine an action that is clear and proportionate."

At about the same time the oversight board was making its determination public, Trump announced that he would be launching his own social media platform.

Back in the nineties, during the birth and early growth of what became known as "social media," the emergence of instant messaging and its accompanying immediate gratification apparently started shifting the habits and rewired the minds of tens of millions of Internet users. People started getting used to the fact that they didn't have to wait for something to happen. No doubt thousands of fast-food restaurants had to innovate new efficiencies to keep up with the new demand to be quick. They had to shorten wait times for drive-through customers (who were made more impatient than ever by the Internet's amazing speed) to be served their unhealthy food quicker than ever. Jack (in the Box) be nimble, Jack be quick.

Things really started to change in the 2000s with the creation of social media. Most notable was the instant popularity of Myspace after its release (it dominated social media from about 2005-2008), followed soon after by Facebook and Twitter. You can even go back to Napster, which was founded in 1999. It allowed users to download as much music as they wanted for a nominal monthly fee. No longer did you have to go out and buy CDs from brick-and-mortar retailers (remember Tower Records, anyone?). The big kid on the block in the earliest days of social media was Myspace. Through Myspace, people became addicted to caring about what other people thought of them. Bullying in the digital world was created by accident. In an instant you could let whoever was important to you know if he or she had somehow upset you. And in so doing, you could knock the person down a peg on the totem pole of peer popularity. The "Top Friends" list might as well have been a social credit system like you would see in China. Myspace's success would eventually be surpassed by that of Facebook.

Facebook was founded at Harvard University, where its cofounders, Mark Zuckerberg and Eduardo Saverin, were enrolled. In the beginning, it was purely social—just a means of enabling college students to talk with one another. You couldn't even get onto it unless you had a university email address. Something changed, though, and its users wanted more connection, more speed, more instant gratification. Social media's biggest gift of this was also their greatest issue: it gave every single person an opportunity to be heard globally. Whatever they thought, wanted, or felt could be communicated to conceivably hundreds of millions of other Facebook users around the world. Instantly. Who could have ever imagined such power?

The company's founding, early growth, and apparent greed—the story ends with one cofounder pitted against the other in a lawsuit—are depicted in the movie *The Social Network*. A hundred years from now, *The Social Network* will likely be viewed as the story of how the seed that destroyed everything was planted.

Social media added the straw that broke the camel's back of America's compass. Ask yourself: How could we as free

Americans end up allowing our government to lock us down, keep us in our homes, and allow fear to run rampant in our society as it has during the covid-19 pandemic that started in early 2020? I know why you allowed it to happen. Fear. Everything that has happened over the past sixty years has led to one thing: *fear* made you do it, plain and simple.

How did we get to this point? It's been a gradual process over the last six decades or so, as I just outlined. For the past fifty or sixty years, we've been heading to where we are now, a point where individualism is no longer important to Americans. It's no longer important to work hard and work for what you need, where each of us earn our just rewards and individual work ethic and achievement gets noticed and celebrated. Not so much now. Today it's just follow the crowd and don't stick your neck out. Outliers need not apply. One person doesn't wear a mask, we all do. Step out of line and risk the ridicule and wrath of others. It's the same thing whether you are a millionaire or not. Yet where we are as a society is exactly what we wished for. We wished to have the same things as soon as we got out of college that our parents had to work thirty or forty years for to get. We wished for the ability to have things instantly at our disposal. Along with that, we wished for less interaction. So it is that the breakdown of the nuclear family and of marriage, accompanied by the rising divorce rate, is off the charts. We wished for that because at the end of the day, nobody wants to be locked down with any one person at any one given time anymore.

Many of us today—society as a whole, in fact—are living with the delusion that we "deserve better and that we deserve more." That is the outgrowth of wishing for something. But I've got news for you: the idea that we deserve *anything* is flawed. It's a terrible idea because, realistically, we don't deserve anything but a big old fiery pit at the end of this life on Earth. It's only through the love and saving grace of Jesus Christ that we even have the *opportunity* to be something more after we die. But as a whole, there were those who two thousand years ago wanted to get rid of Jesus, too (and some like those are still around today). Why? Because Jesus and God hold us accountable, just as parents and other authority figures used to do before the decades-long crumbling of our moral fabric I described earlier. Jesus and God aren't there just to make us feel good and dish up whatever we want instantly. If you are among the masses who have such a notion, please explain to me where you got it from and what justifies it. I'd really like to know. Jesus and God make us realize that we're doing stuff we're not supposed to be doing. God and Christianity in the school, in the workplace, in the home reminded us of the very things we were doing wrong. But it's what we want to do, so we have to get God out of here. *We wished for that.* People don't realize that, but that was what we did.

Remember: be careful what you wish for.

I'm holding up a yellow caution flag and saying you need to be careful because you just might get it. Beware: *having* is sometimes nowhere near as appealing as *wanting.* What we have now is a large group of individuals (numbering in the tens, if not hundreds, of millions) who believe that we are no longer *E pluribus unum* but "me, myself, and I." "What can I get out of this society?" they ask. "What can America do for me? You mean to tell me I don't have to work? I can stay home and make bare minimum, which qualifies me for free health care, free cell phone, free Internet, free cable? Some programs even help pay for my house." During the covid-19 lockdowns there were people making more from unemployment than they had been making at work. The most dangerous thing of all is not desiring *equality* but confusing it with *equity*. Everybody wants everything, to have the same things as everyone else—if not more. This mass mindset has been engineered in this country by pushing the idea of a racial divide. The Democrats are just as guilty as they accuse the Republicans of being. The truth is that not everyone is entitled to the same things. Not even close. Everyone is not going to be the best at what it is they're doing, and they need to know that not everyone's going to succeed in life.

The biggest lie we've ever been told is that in America, you can be whatever you want to be. That is simply not true. What that motto should say is that in America, you have the *opportunity* to accomplish whatever you set your mind to along with the reality that you might fail. And most likely you *will fail*! Join the club. I have failed so many times in my life. I have come up short more times than I can count. I have hurt friends and loved ones and almost destroyed my own business. This is the way *real* life goes. I'm also willing to bet a load of cash that more than half of the truly successful people in this country have failed at something fairly significant along the way, in most cases probably more than once. And those eighth- and ninth-place ribbons you were awarded in school—essentially for just being present and participating—won't buy you squat in the grown-up world. All those worthless ribbons do for you is perpetuate the myth that you have achieved greatness solely by trying. Uh-huh. Nope. Doesn't work that way. Or at least it *shouldn't* work that way.

For twenty years the US Army had a recruiting motto that said, "Be all you can be." It did not say, "Be all you *want* to be." There's a huge difference. There's no guarantee that you're going to make it. There's no guarantee that you're going to establish a multimillion-dollar company. There's no guarantee that you're going to be an astronaut. What if something is medically wrong with you that you don't know about? The astronaut program has very strict physical, emotional, and psychological standards. It is not an entitlement.

It used to be—that you can be whatever you want to be in terms of accomplishment. It's even easier today to be what you want to be just by declaring it so. Yet another layer of the absurdity of our entitlement society. I'm talking about how you can has turned into "You can literally be whatever you want to be." You can be a boy, a girl, a dolphin. Who can argue with you at this point? Where would you begin? It's outrageous. The powers of political correctness will shut up whatever objection you might have to the subject. The actor Ellen Page comes out and says she's no longer a lesbian, she's now Elliot Page. She's now a straight male who is married to a lesbian. That would be a riddle in any science fiction novel, for sure! Facebook currently says that there are seventy-two genders. Is this living the American dream?

We are supposed to believe that there is no God; there are multiple gods. We are also supposed to believe that when you die nothing happens afterward, which in itself is a belief. The idea that you believe in nothing is an insane concept that simply isn't true. You literally cannot believe in nothing, because if you believe in nothing you believe in something; it's just that your something happens to be nothing.

You ask me: How did we get here? I just told you how.

I can progress in my business. I can turn my business from a $5 million business into a $20 million business. But know this: progress isn't always what's best for society or your family. In reference to that difference in running a company I just mentioned, growing it from $5 million a year to $20 million a year—think of the time spent away from family, the stress involved, and so on. Is that really what's best, just so you can have more money? That's a question every single person has to answer. The problem is that most people will say yes and worry less about the actual relationship toll growing the company has on you and your spouse—or the relationship you do not have with your kids.

I am pro-entrepreneur. All the way. People need to understand, though, that if you are going to make $100 million a year, there is no such thing as a forty-hour workweek. There is no hundred-hour workweek. It's 24/7 all the time, every single day. You are never off. Even when you are asleep, the engine is running, commerce is happening somewhere in the world. You miss your kids' games. You are not home all the time, if much at all. You miss date nights with your spouse.

There are pros and cons to everything. We are living with a generation that thinks there is nothing but pros to everything and whatever that "everything" encompasses should be gifted to them at the max level, at the max benefit. When I say be careful what you wish for because you just might get it, keep in mind that the entire past sixty-plus years has been about making America more prosperous, more self-gratifying, and easier. What it has produced is individuals who no longer care about America as a whole; they only care about themselves.

There is nothing innately wrong with wanting to make life easier. In fact, it's a good mindset. But we've seen something time and time again. It's an old tale: A person comes from nothing and builds immense wealth. The kids live with that immense wealth. The kids don't do anything with their lives, and in many cases, they just mooch off society. Then their kids have an absentee mother or father who won't do anything for them because they are emotionally unavailable, concerned only about themselves. Then the cycle repeats itself.

Good times create weak men. Hard times create strong men. It's one of the most basic things that you can possibly imagine.

We are now in a situation where our country is not our country anymore. America is not America anymore. We are not the only ones who feel it. China feels it; it sees it. So do Russia, North Korea, and others. Many of the countries in the Middle East—they know. They're not stupid. America is not the same America as before. In the grand scheme of things, a country is only as powerful as its citizens. It doesn't matter how powerful the president is or the dictator is; if the people are powerful, the government fears the people and acts right.

If the people are weak, the government becomes powerful because it no longer fears the people.

This takes me to George Washington, the United States' first president, who is often referred to as the father of our country. There was something he once said, when he was General George Washington, that goes with romanticizing about how great America has done through the years. Our history books, at least the ones I studied when I was in school more than fifteen years ago, tell us that the Revolutionary War was a magical moment for the colonies. At the time we had a total population of around 2.6 million to 2.7 million people, and everyone just decided one day that they wanted to declare independence from British rule. In so many words, we are told, they proclaimed, "We want to be our own nation, and that's what we're going to do."

That's not true at all. In fact, it was the opposite—not even close to the unanimity that the history books suggest. It was probably closer to 55 to 45 percent, barely in favor of those who wanted to declare and fight for independence over the others who wanted to keep bending the knee to King George III. Out of that 2.6 or so million people, maybe 10 percent actually took up arms and fought to win the Revolutionary War. What a lot of people today probably don't realize is how many years the war dragged on (eight!) and the fact that there were many ups and downs. Numerous times during those eight years, we wondered if we were even going to win the war. Great doubt slipped into our collective mindset from time to time.

There was something spot on that General Washington wrote to a friend during one of those times of unspoken great doubt on a night when he and all of his troops were freezing and were out of food: "The reflection upon my Situation, & that of this Army, produces many an uneasy hour when all around me are wrapped in Sleep. Few People know the Predicament we are In." What Washington was thinking that night, while looking around at everyone under his command asleep, was that they had no idea how much trouble they were in then, how close they were to losing the battle.

We are in the exact same situation in America right now. So many people are asleep, snuggled up in their beds at night or spending private moments in their closed-in garages, without any communication with the outside world except through Facebook, Instagram, whatever news outlet they choose to believe, or whatever TV shows they watch that are telling them what and how to think or feel. They have no clue as to the predicament we are in and how close we are to losing America as it was meant to be.

Be careful what you wish for; you just might get it.

Two

FEAR IS CONTAGIOUS

*"The hard truth and data are this . . . fear consumes
faster than any virus ever could."*

Congratulations! If you are vertical, breathing, and reading this book, you survived the worst that covid-19 could throw at you. Whether you tested positive or not, showed symptoms or not, faithfully wore your mask and kept six feet between yourself and others or not, you made it this far.

That's the good news.

Now for the bad news (this is where it gets scary).

You're never going back.

Yes, I said it. You are *never* going back. At least, that is what they want for us. You will never again work in an office filled with employees or go into a nightclub, restaurant, subway, airplane, movie theater, church, sports stadium—you name it—without a certain amount of trepidation. Like tens of millions of others, you will continue to walk through life fixated on the possibility that there still is a microscopic infectious superbug lurking nearby. It has your name on it and is itching to jump into your unguarded mouth or crawl up an exposed nostril.

Forget what normal used to be. We can now call that "the old normal." That is, the way things used to be back when we were young—you know, back in February 2020—when words such as *pandemic*, *symptomatic*, and *hydroxychloroquine* were kept safely locked away in someone else's vocabulary, not ours. The old days are gone. We now occupy a new normal, and even then, it's not really "new" anymore. The new normal sprouted up right before our eyes, nose, and mouth, and now it is just plain ordinary. Our not-so-new-anymore normal is one in which you keep your masks, plastic shields, or other preferred face covering easily accessible at arm's length, maybe for the rest of your life.

Does this make you sad? Does it make you angry? Do you feel another wave of fear about to wash up on your toes? Would it help if you talked about it with someone?

The vaccines that came to us at warp speed (the vaccine-development program was named Operation Warp Speed) have apparently worked. So far, no one—as best as I can tell—has turned into a flesh-eating zombie after receiving his or her shots. If that did happen somewhere, our government did its usual bang-up job of keeping the vital information from its citizens. That's not the sort of thing that even a loose-lipped Joe Biden would unwittingly make public near a hot mic. One truth is that the numbers of positive tests, hospitalizations, and covid-19-related deaths—as reported—started falling around January 2021, thanks to the vaccines that the Donald Trump administration produced for us. Our capacity to succumb to state-engineered fear, though, has not subsided. We remain in a sticky situation, a society that has undergone a pandemic-induced paradigm shift.

So, we can breathe easier now (taking off that annoying mask certainly helps). There's nothing left to fear, right? Not so fast. Let's ponder a few hypotheticals. What if the now-dormant virus inside your body has a trick up its sleeve and mutates enough to light the fuse on another covid-19 outbreak—one impervious to the existing vaccines? Or what happens if, say, as a random example, Chinese scientists concoct a new variant of coronavirus that is more transmissible and deadlier than covid-19? Then they have it delivered overnight express to target zones of an unsuspecting populace, in effect confirming that World War III is at hand. Then we will have a weaponized virus threatening to bring the rest of the world to its knees (joining the college and professional athletes already there).

In the United States, fear spreads faster than a virus itself. China, Russia, and other nations know this, and they are watching and listening. Is a Biden-led nation (or one led by his successor) ready to handle what might come next from abroad? If the first two months of Biden's presidency showed us anything, it's that countries do not respect him or us. Within the same week, North Korea, China, and Russia basically slapped the United States in the face, and he did nothing. Why? Because they knew they could, that's why! There's plenty more to fear from over there than a killer virus, but that is for another time.

A quick rundown of what happened during that Hell Week (actually, it spans ten days, but who's counting?) with North Korea, China, and Russia:

- On March 18, 2021, an official allied with the Kremlin threatened some form of retaliation against the United States while demanding an apology or explanation from Biden regarding the latter's description of Russian president Vladimir Putin as a "soulless killer."

- On the weekend of March 20–21, 2021, North Korea fired multiple short-range missiles right after criticizing the Biden administration for its moving ahead with joint military exercises with South Korea. Pesty North Korean leader Kim Jong-un was at it again, testing American resolve. Apparently, our enemies hate us just as much without Donald Trump in office. Even the left-leaning *Washington Post* threw a log onto the fire, making room in its coverage to quote Kim Yo-jong, the North Korean leader's sister, taking a swipe at Biden, reportedly saying that if the Biden administration "wants to sleep in peace for the coming four years, it had better refrain from causing a stink."

- On the same day (March 27, 2021) that China effectively spit in the United States' eye by signing a twenty-five-year "cooperation agreement" with Iran, China's Ministry of Foreign Affairs placed sanctions on the chair and vice chair of the United States Commission on International Religious Freedom. At least this shows that it's possible to put "China" and "religious freedom" in the same sentence.

We've been down a similar path before, one that forever altered the core tenets and routine practices and habits that determine how we live our lives. And we never went back. Twenty years ago, it was the terrorist attacks of September 11, 2001, that hit New York City and Washington, DC, accompanied by a terrorist-hijacked jet planted into a field in western Pennsylvania forced to the ground by a small army of brave, resourceful passengers on flight 93. The tragic events of 9/11 are still showing their presence, most noticeably in the tightened security at airports and more metal detectors in government buildings and offices across America.

We're not going back. Some things are simply that life changing. Some "aftereffects" of an event or a virus never really go away.

I remember when I first started hearing about the coronavirus while watching the news and heard the first snippets about this virus. One thing we heard clearly: the thing had somehow originated in China; Wuhan, China, to be precise. It wasn't the first time we had heard about bad things coming out of China. When the Devil fell from Heaven, I'm pretty sure he landed in China, where he planted the secretive, cunning Chinese Communist Party; nothing good has ever come from it. It is a horrible national government that casts a pall over the entire nation, although, of course, that is not meant as an indictment of its citizens in general. Yes, NBA and LeBron James, I said it. China is a *horrible country*, especially when it comes to things like human rights and its oppressive sweat shops, utilized by the likes of the American athletic shoe-maker Nike. China's leaders relish this! The government there relishes the fact that it has concentration camps and sweat-shops. Most Americans, at least those who are beholden to political correctness, keep dancing around the topic of China, scared to say anything bad about the Communist country. I'm not talking about Chinese Americans, only what we prop-erly label as China—or what used to be called Red China—the actual Chinese Communist Party, which is running that (crap) show over there.

It was Monday, March 1, 2020, eve of Super Tuesday. I was in Charlotte, North Carolina, invited there to be a special guest at one of Donald Trump's "Keep America Great" rallies. I was standing at the back getting ready to greet the president. I had met him several times before, but it was the first time I had ever heard a Secret Service officer tell me something like "With this thing going on with China, nobody is going to shake hands with the president today, just as a precaution." At this point, I think there were only about twenty-five confirmed cases of it in the United States, but President Trump's detail was being extra careful. They made all of us—we were in the back part of the convention center in Charlotte—sanitize our hands even though we weren't going to be shaking the pres-ident's hand. When we finally got up onstage with the pres-ident, he recognized me right away and shook my hand. He and I talked for a couple of minutes, he shook my wife's hand and took photos with us, and everything was back to good.

Soon Trump went out onto the stage, and it was one of the most electric things I've ever witnessed in my life: thirty or forty thousand people just losing their minds over President Trump. We listened to his message; then we went home that night and didn't think much else about the hand sanitizer and shaking his hand. Two weeks later, though—by now it was mid-March—it was a different story. I had to go down to Charleston, South Carolina, for a speaking event put on by the organization Turning Point USA. It was around that time that everything started to change. More and more people were getting sick, and we started hearing things about Donald Trump shutting down flights from China. At the same time, House speaker Nancy Pelosi, Representative Alexandria Ocasio-Cortez (AOC), and even Joe Biden, still known only as the former vice president, were calling President Trump a racist, a bigot, a China-phobe, everything you can imagine. I remember seeing a news clip in which Pelosi was in San Francisco's Chinatown, encouraging people to come out, saying that there was nothing to fear. Yet we seem to have either forgotten that or simply refuse to talk about it.

At one point I had considered not even going to the event in Charleston, but that was because my grandfather—the man who raised me—had just passed away. Normally, I would have canceled and gone to the funeral but because everyone was freaking out about the virus, I wasn't even allowed to lay the most prominent male figure in my life to rest. That hurt and I was feeling really conflicted, plus I was angry. So, I thought,

You know what? I might as well go to this thing. Nobody knows what's going on with this coronavirus [most people were still a way away from calling the disease covid-19] *or if it's actually an existential threat. Whatever is going to happen is going to happen, so I might just as well go.*

To this day, at least the last time I checked, there's a video on the Internet in which I presented a list of all the things you were more likely to die of than the coronavirus early in the days of the pandemic. One of the ones on the list was constipation, which I thought was really funny. So, I made a joke about it, saying that you were more likely to be run over by a lawn mower than die of the coronavirus. Then the coronavirus started to hit more and more, and that was when people really started to freak out. College basketball tournaments were abruptly canceled, as were festivals, parades, and civic events throughout the country. Even the eagerly awaited St. Patrick's Day celebrations were canceled, leaving organizers sobbing into their green beer. Churches, movie theaters, schools, colleges, and universities were closed, on and on.

Untold thousands of dominos were all falling at the same time. Major League Baseball suspended its spring training just a little over a week before the scheduled start of the season. One of the holdouts was the National Basketball Association, which had only a month or so left in its regular season before the playoffs were to start. Then something strange happened. At midweek, the Utah Jazz and Oklahoma City Thunder were about to tip off for their game in Oklahoma City. The starting lineups had been announced and the game was moments away from starting, when suddenly Donnie Strack, a Thunder vice president, came running onto the court to stop the game just as the lead officials were about to start the game with the traditional jump ball. The news, as delivered by the horseless version of Paul Revere (Strack), wasn't good. One of Oklahoma City's players, Rudy Gobert, who had stayed in the team's locker room because he wasn't feeling well, had just tested positive for covid-19. And just like that, the NBA season came to a screeching halt. The players at the Jazz-Thunder game were pulled off the court, the fans in attendance were kept in the dark for thirty minutes, and then, *poof!*, the season was stopped (to be played out in the summer and early fall). All that within a matter of about an hour, maybe two.

Showtime had left the building, replaced by unchallenged fear.

The public reaction to the quickly spreading pandemic was swift and ferocious. Everybody raced to the local grocery store to stock up on masks, toilet paper (seriously, do people *eat* the stuff?), hand sanitizer, water, and Pop-Tarts. Oh, and don't forget eggs, milk, and cookies. Almost everything you can imagine.

While all that chaos was going on in stores across America, I said to myself, *I'm still going to do it. I'm going to go head down to Charleston*, and I did, driving there with my business partner alongside me. Once there, it was about an hour before I was to go onstage and speak when coverage went live to President Trump in the Rose Garden at the White House. He was surrounded by officials, experts, and corporate leaders talking about how serious the virus is, how it was not to be taken lightly, and how our lives were going to change. I immediately got onto the phone to call my office and spoke to some folks there, such as my producer, telling them how it was going to change everything. I also said I was going to go ahead with my speech, and we would figure all this out, and how to react to it, when I got back.

It turned out to be the least attended speech I had ever done. People were supposed to be there in the thousands, but it ended up being just a couple hundred showing up, as many canceled. You could tell that people everywhere were afraid. My message at that time was that now is not the time to live in fear; it is a time to live in the truth of what we know. Looking back, it's ironic that I said what I did, because more than a year later, as I write this, we're still not living in the truth of what we know. As nasty as the symptoms have been for some who tested positive for covid-19, a year later the survival rate remains more than over 99 percent, and *that* is the truth. That is what we know.

When I got home from Charleston, I was not so much afraid of the virus as I was for how other people were going to react and what they might do in this state of mass fear. What are we going to do, I wondered, if all the hoarding wackos here go out and buy everything up, leaving many people unable to even get the basics of what they need? What are we going to do if the grocery stores are shut down and places like CVS, Walmart, and Walgreens close down, making it nearly impossible for folks who absolutely need to pick up, say, their prescriptions to do so?

Thankfully, I live in a red state. South Carolina was one of the last states to mandate any kind of covid-19-related restrictions. Looking around the rest of the country and the world, though, I saw practically every other state obediently fall into line without question, locking everything down. Many people's jobs were put on hold, most of those whose jobs could be performed at home. Many of those who couldn't take their work home with them were deemed to be essential workers. Meanwhile, workplaces had to be reengineered and reconfigured to separate workers from one another, while both workers and clients were still instructed to wear masks, maintain six feet of distance from other people, avoid shaking hands, and wash their hands thoroughly as needed. Whether you worked in an office or at home, most likely you had at least one bottle of hand sanitizer at arm's length—if you were fortunate to be able to find any after the overeager hoarders had emptied the store shelves.

It took a few weeks to catch on, but the most readily evident sign that we were now in a pandemic and people were being treated like cattle was the widespread wearing of masks in public. They were everywhere, with few exceptions. In multiple episodes of my show—you can go all the way back to the very beginning of the pandemic in the United States—I said it was the start of something that would never go away. Either the coronavirus was an existential virus that would kill us all and none of this stuff would matter anyway, or it was going to prove to be a massive overreaction based on fear. Maybe it was some kind of weird experiment to see exactly what the feds can get away with making us do? I said, in so many words, "The mask is more than just a mask. The mask is all about control; it's about obedience. It will eventually become a social status–type symbol." I said from day one that the mask will never go away in America. We will be just like China and Japan, where half the population wears masks in mass gatherings and half the population doesn't. It will become a fashion statement. They will figure out ways to turn it into fashion to make money off the American people: find or create your own personalized mask, putting on it whatever you want to show off, maybe your dog or cat or your favorite movie or TV character. Businesses have literally been created with massive multimillion-dollar grants and backers to become face mask creators and/or distributors. Prominent apparel lines, such as Hanes, were now making masks. I own an apparel business, and we tossed around the idea of creating our own line of masks. We even launched a giveaway that included masks. However, I refused to produce them because they go against what I believe and what I represent on my show. It would have been hypocritical of me. There's nothing like using a handy pandemic to create fear in people and then get them to face that fear (no pun intended) with a nifty-looking mask.

Covid-19 has created jobs and new revenue streams for everybody except the people who already had jobs. Rich people created new revenue streams for themselves. Joe Blow, who works at AT&T, doesn't have the money to start a business that requires an assembly line and a mass distribution apparatus. Keep in mind, too, that most of them aren't even the medical masks used in health care settings—they are just made from cloth no different from what's used to make the T-shirt I'm now wearing. Yet all of a sudden, this is what's going to save your life, what's going to protect you and others?

Honestly, just walk with your hand over your mouth. You will achieve the same amount of "protection."

Now, I need to make one thing crystal clear: this book is not a conspiracy book. I'm not saying that the virus isn't real. In fact, I know firsthand how real the virus is. On September 28, 2020—a day I'll never forget—I woke up not feeling well. I immediately knew that something was wrong. It was a feeling I had never felt before. I have had the worst the flu has to offer in my life, but this one was different. For ten straight days I had an intense fever. I could barely move, could not eat, could barely breathe. I lost twenty pounds in ten days. Even at my weakest moment I began to briefly ponder, *What if this does take me out? What if I was wrong?*

In the end, I wasn't wrong. There is no doubt that I had it pretty bad, but my entire family also had it. They got over it like it was nothing. Many others are over it with mild cold symptoms in two or three days. I know the coronavirus can be a very bad virus for some people; I was one of them. But I still think that every single bit of this overreaction stuff, with the mainstream media obsessing over it and all the mask stuff and mandating shutdowns and closures, is bull. Every last bit of everything we are doing in light of the coronavirus is nothing more than BS, and in that regard, we will get into the hypocrisy of government, the hypocrisy of leaders. Everything surrounding the coronavirus tells us that *hindsight really is 2020!* This is irony at its best.

The fear is what's contagious.

As I stated in my first book, one of my first memories as a child involves fear—the fear that I felt. My first memory of fear was the time I was in my parents' first home and couldn't find my father or mother. It's amazing how a 1,200-square-foot house seems gigantic when you're young. I couldn't find my parents, and I remember just how the intense fear consumed me. I remember running outside and not being able to find them, then running to the neighbors' house, banging on their door, and telling them, "I can't find my mom. I'm here by myself, terrified." It turned out that my mom had actually been in the laundry room the whole time and I had forgotten to look there.

I had a similar experience with one of my sons in a hotel. We were pushing two carts of luggage. When we got to the elevator—which had to be one of the smallest elevators ever created in the history of the world—we found that only one of us could fit in it at a time. So I pushed my son Gunnar, who was nine at the time, in first and hit the button for the floor that we were on. I told him that I was going to be right behind him in the next elevator. "You get out of the elevator," I said. "Then stand right there and wait on me."

After his door closed, I hit the call button to get my elevator; it took about thirty seconds to show up. I got in, went up to the second floor, the elevator door opened, no Gunnar. No cart, no nothing. I stood there and looked around knowing that there was no way somebody had stolen him that quickly. So, I hit the call button to go up. My elevator, the same one I just rode up in, opened first, but I didn't get in. Instead, I hit the down call button, thinking it would open the other elevator that my son had been in, but that one didn't open up. It's gone, it had left that floor. So, I left my cart on the second floor, went down to the front desk. I asked, "Do you have cameras on the floors? I can't find my son, who just went up in the other elevator. Do you have cameras in the elevator?" The people at the desk said, "No, we only have it in the main lobby."

I started to panic, fearing that my son was stuck somewhere on the wrong floor or between floors in the elevator. The woman at the front desk got onto the phone to call her manager, and I started thinking, *we're going to have to call the fire department*. Gunnar didn't have a phone; he didn't have anything. I had no way to reach him.

In near desperation, I told the front-desk person that I was going to go up one more time and check again. I stepped into the same elevator I had just come down in—the one he was in still wouldn't open because it was somewhere else. I went up to the second floor in "my" elevator, and standing right next to my cart was Gunnar, bawling his eyes out. Come to find out, the bags that had gone up with him had fallen out of the cart and he couldn't get them out of the elevator. He had looked outside of his elevator when he arrived at the floor for which I had originally pushed the button inside his elevator, and I wasn't there yet. So he'd gone right back down. We had literally been passing and missing each other the entire time like some sort of comedy routine, but I wasn't laughing. Gunnar was consumed by as much fear as I was, thinking I had left him. As I say, fear spreads faster than a virus ever could.

I am a bit of a hypochondriac (if you listen to my show, you know this is something I struggle with daily) and fear getting mortally sick. Cancer runs in my family. My mom had it, my grandfather had it, and my dad had it. So my chances aren't that great. They all made it through their bouts with cancer, but if I don't feel right, I automatically think I have cancer: *This is it, I'm going to die.* A family history of a particular health issue can be a scary thing, and I admit that I am a hypochondriac in that regard. Even though I've learned to live with it (sort of), not let it consume every waking moment, it can still hit me like a truckload of bricks at such times. That's when I end up in a depressive state where I can't do anything. It can also be argued that that is why I push so hard, so often. I have always feared that I don't have as much time as everyone else. This is actually common in men my age, but that knowledge doesn't help me calm down most days.

Anyway, back to the point!

The covid-19 pandemic has not been an existential threat to society. I said so from the very beginning and got "fact-checked" by every single one of Facebook's censor police for it, but I will say that it has been a world-changing-forever event. It's not because the virus was deadly or that it was spreading at such a rapid pace that nobody knew what it was. We knew what it was, and we felt the fear of it that spread across America and led the shutdowns of businesses, the panic buying at grocery stores, the postponement and cancellation of sports contests, and so forth. To put it into perspective, consider the Spanish flu, which lasted from February 1918 to April 1919 at a time when medicine and medical treatment were nothing like they are today. Nearly 750,000 Americans and 50 million people worldwide died of the flu, with about one-third of the world's population stricken during that pandemic. Yet America didn't stop back then; it kept on going. There was nothing about not being able to see your family or "You can't go there" and "You can't do that." There was no football or baseball being canceled. They understood enough at the time to know you can't shut everything down, because if they had, it would have been all over for us.

That's not how it is in America today, where fear has taken over *everything* we do. We are so afraid of everything. Forget the virus; there's plenty else to put us into and keep us in a state of fear at the drop of a hat. We are so afraid of offending people, for starters. Taking offense over something said or written about you is a choice, and Americans have made it an obsession. People are now afraid to say what they really think and feel because someone will see or hear it and twist it into an excuse for taking offense; it's another form of phony self-inflicted victimization.

Face it, many of us are just thin-skinned versions of what Americans used to be. In the world of social media, we are afraid that some dude on a sofa two thousand miles away we don't know and will most likely never meet might post a comment on a thread we started that is mean—and that bothers us? It scares us! Actually it does more than scare us, it dictates our actions every single day. We become consumed by the fear of what someone online may say or do. We have gone from being a nation with fifteen-year-olds lying about their age so they could enter the service and storm the beaches of Normandy, knowing that we would most likely they would die, to now being a national collection of social media users afraid to post a candid comment on the Internet about what we believe and feel because somebody might say something mean back at us. We are afraid to tell others the truth. Take, for instance, the topic of gender identification. Mention that on Facebook, and now you've opened up a can of worms. Chances are all sorts of responses will come back at you, some supportive, some in opposition, some calling you names and maybe even one or two disparaging you or even threatening you in some manner. This stuff can grow like weeds in a heartbeat, leaving you wondering what you just got yourself into. *Could this person threatening me somehow get my address? Do I need to buy a gun for home protection?*

By the way, just in case you were wondering where I stand on the subject: there are not dozens of genders out there, as some will insist; there are two! And *only* two. There, I said it. Putting a number on *There are only two genders!* That's an example of how some folks at the end of the day will say that there are no constants out there. This is not true, obviously; of course there are constants out there. We just don't like to accept that things actually have rules and social norms that we should live by. Taxes, death, opinions, and *two genders*! Those are things you can always count on! Even if someone doesn't want to live that way. We want to live as if there are no truths and no constants. It makes the world easier to deal with. People fear actually having to deal with what they are and who they are and trying to find validation, the lack of which terrifies them.

Fear has taken over the church, too. The church is not what it used to be. It is now so afraid of offending its members,

of losing tithes and offerings, that many ministers, preach-
ers, and evangelists are now carefully crafting their messages from the pulpit to better suit the ears and expectations
of socially awakened congregations. Part of the evolution of
church messaging is no doubt inspired by Eric Mason's 2018
book, *Woke Church: An Urgent Call for Christians in America
to Confront Racism and Injustice.* In it, Mason, who is black
and identified by his publisher as the founder and lead pastor
of Epiphany Fellowship in Philadelphia, is apparently calling
on churches to join with the likes of Black Lives Matter (and
perhaps antifa, too?) to apply properly interpreted biblical
passages to help in the fight against injustice and oppression
targeted at African Americans.

Following is an excerpt from Amazon's description of Dr.
Church and his book:

Like the Old Testament prophets, and more recent
prophetic voices like Frederick Douglass, Dr. Eric
Mason calls the evangelical church to a much-needed
reckoning. In a time when many feel confused, com-
placent, or even angry, he challenges the church to:

Be Aware—to understand that the issue of justice
is not a black issue, it's a kingdom issue. To learn how
the history of racism in America and in the church
has tainted our witness to a watching world.

Be Redemptive—to grieve and lament what we
have lost and to regain our prophetic voice, calling
the church to remember our gospel imperative to promote justice and mercy.

Be Active—to move beyond polite, safe conversations about reconciliation and begin to set things aright for our soon-coming King, who will be looking for a WOKE CHURCH."

Then there's this: the creation of a new Methodist denomination known as "the Liberation Methodist Connexion (LMX)," which has been described as a "socially progressive denomination that will reimagine what it means to follow Jesus." Wow! That sounds exciting. I wonder if Jesus himself knows about this. Of course he does. One thing for certain: LMX is not to be confused with orthodox Christianity.

"We seek not answers that lead us to correct doctrines as to why we suffer. We seek correct actions, correct praxis, where God sustains us during the unanswerable questions," says Reverend Althea Spencer-Miller, an LMX leader quoted on Religion News Service. According to David Closson, writing for Family Research Council in December 2020, the creation of LMX falls into line with a tentative agreement among representatives of the United Methodist Church to split over "fundamental differences" related to church doctrine on matters such as homosexuality, same-sex marriage, and the ordination of clergy who identify as gay. A formal vote on whether to split the denomination was supposed to take place in 2020 but was delayed to fall 2021 because of the covid-19 pandemic.

So the message from the pulpit is watered down, often sounding more like a motivational feel-good seminar than scriptural truth. Feel-good preaching is so much more palatable to the ears of church attendees than fire and brimstone, even if significantly toned down. Here is a simple question: Where are our pastors today? Many are living in fear, afraid to take on the powerful forces of political correctness. Socialism may threaten to destroy our country, but I promise that "woke Christianity" will kill it first!

We are allowing fear to trample on our constitutional rights as Americans, while we are being told we can't open up our own business or go to work, or we can't see our extended families, or we can't worship where and when we want to? Where are you in terms of being under God's authority? The Constitution was written under God's authority. The church is supposed to be the most powerful entity in the country outside of the people themselves.

The biggest thing I hate is the separation of church and state argument, which says that the church and the state should never have anything to do with each other. People make that argument out of fear. They also make it out of confusion of what it was supposed to mean in the first place. The separation of church and state was made to keep the government out of the church; it was not made to keep the church out of government! The church is 100 percent supposed to be influential in the creation of laws and regulations in this land, but people started twisting what the separation of church and state actually means. Why? Because real churches uphold biblical truth, which sometimes makes people feel bad, even accused of sin, for not abiding by what God calls for them to do or not do. That's why "feel-good" churches are in vogue. People living in fear now attack churches and go after them to try to knock them out of business. People don't want the church reminding them that they're not living the way they're supposed to be living.

What's worst is that "woke" pastors are perpetuating this state of affairs. There are also pastors who are preaching the prosperity gospel, when they are the ones living the most prosperous lives, holed up in million-dollar homes and flying around the country in private jets, supported by thousands upon thousands of congregants. All of these pastors are *not* preaching from a point of authority through God and the Bible. They're preaching from the point of authority of likes and followers on social media such as Facebook and Instagram. Again, socialism might kill this country, but I promise you, woke Christianity will kill all of us first.

It's all about fear! The church is failing because it fears offending its members. Show me a place in the Bible where Jesus cared about hurting anybody's feelings. He didn't. He just told the truth. He loved everyone, but expressing love sometimes means hurting other people's feelings. I would argue that the people who love people the most are the people who are willing to hurt your feelings because they care about you that much. Jesus cared about your soul. He couldn't care less what your emotions said in the finite terms of the blip on the radar that we are alive on this earth. Jesus was about truth, and the truth is that the truth hurts!

Our entire world operates around fear. We have police officers who can't do their jobs because they're afraid that someone is going to record them, paint them as bad guys, so they risk losing their jobs, going to jail themselves, and not being able to provide for their families. They even risk their own lives by hesitating in a job where split-second decisions mean life and death! That is the unstated goal of activist groups such as antifa and Black Lives Matter—they are not seeking justice and fairness for minorities, they are looking to induce and stoke fear in our country while tearing our country down, and at some level they are succeeding.

There are doctors who believe that they have found creative, alternative means of fighting covid-19 who are too afraid to speak up. They're afraid they'll be chastised and lose their jobs and licenses, which means that they would not be able to practice anymore or take care of their own families.

Fear is taking over every aspect of who we are and what we do. Music has changed. Movies have changed. The way we interact in the office has changed. People can't tell a joke anymore. That's because they fear other people's opinions of them, and that now rules who we are as a society. One of my favorite shows of all time is *The Office*. I personally want there to be a new season so bad, but Steve Carell, who plays Michael Scott, said he would never do it because there is no way they could get away with what they got away with so many years ago. Fear has caused Americans to lie down and say, "Yes, government, we will do whatever you say. Please don't be mad at us." In hindsight, it's hilarious that we would allow our government to close our businesses through fear and put into place mandates that dictate that we're not allowed to work during a pandemic, but then the government can turn around and collect taxes from us with the right to put us into jail or possess our homes and cars if we don't—or are unable to—comply. We *literally* had a US president, Joe Biden, tell Americans that *if* we do what the government wants us to do, we can *possibly* celebrate July Fourth this year! The irony of a sitting US president telling *free* Americans what they can do on Independence Day is not only hilarious but also a sad demonstration of how far the government has fallen away from the *people*! If 10 million people banded together and suddenly refused to pay taxes, just watch—the government would bend the knee and say, "We're sorry. Please pay your taxes. We really need you to do that. We can't arrest ten million people."

Fear is driving us to submit and give up our freedoms as Americans. Fear is the most contagious thing of all. Look at what's going on in regard to playing the national anthem before sporting events. Many athletes kneel out of fear; they fear retribution from people who think that kneeling during the national anthem is a requisite sign of solidarity. "FOMO" is a big slang term right now; it is the acronym for "fear of missing out." Every big company that wants your money is creating this fear right now. They incentivize people by making them think they're going to miss out on something.

I meet so many people every single day who work nine to five in a job they hate, live a life they can't stand every single day, over and over again. They hate every aspect of their unfulfilled lives, knowing that inside they want to do something else, create their own business, or go back to school to prepare for and pursue a different career—but they never make that jump out of fear. That's tragic. That's not what America should be about. They don't make that change, instead coming up with the excuses "Now is not the right time" or "So-and-so's pregnant" or "Once the kids get to a certain age . . ."

My father-in-law once nailed it, saying "A lot of people lack the genetics of not being afraid to fail." In my years, I have discovered that people actually care about something else. It's not so much that they care about failing; it's that they fear other people seeing them fail. They're afraid of what other people will think of them if they don't succeed. People are more afraid of other people's "opinions" than they are of living out their days in a way they can't stand rather than simply taking a chance. The first steps in life are the ones many will never take. Those steps are the ones that show us who we really are. Yet the vast majority of people will never do anything about it. That's the real fear of failure: the fear of others knowing that you did. Entrepreneurs do not fear failure. Better yet, anyone who has changed the world knows that failure is not a bad thing. They know that failure is often part of the process, a building block leading to success; failure is *not* to be feared, on any level.

We live in a generation built by fear. We teach our children to fear instead of to be proud and stand up as Americans—to take chances, to embrace risk. This country became free of British rule by taking a giant risk, a huge leap of faith. Yet in 2020 and 2021, all it took was a virus to make many freedom-loving Americans easily surrender their rights, their freedoms, their liberties as Americans and not even question it? I often wonder what our Founding Fathers would think of us. Would they be proud of the people we have become? I will let you answer that question yourself.

At the present day there are two groups of people: non-maskers and maskers. If they came out tomorrow and said, "Okay, everyone's been vaccinated, covid-19 is no longer a problem," do you really think people who are compliantly wearing masks are just going to stop wearing them? Of course not. Do you really believe people are going to go back to work and say, "We're not worried about covid-19 anymore?" No, this is forever. This is never going to go away.

Within a week of being inaugurated as president, Joe Biden, in late January 2021, signed an executive order stipulating that the Department of Labor, as reported by CNBC, issue guidance that clarifies "workers have a federally guaranteed right to refuse employment that will jeopardize their health and if they do so, they will still qualify for unemployment insurance." Under the previous administration of Donald Trump, it was left to state and local governments to determine what was "suitable work" and what wasn't for the purpose of unemployment compensation eligibility. Biden's executive order changed that, resetting the parameters by making it a federal determination, thus taking it out of the hands of state and local governments. In essence, Biden was promoting guidance that would make it easier—even *expected*—for more people to continue feeding off the government's teat and use covid-19 as an excuse to do so—in effect, to advance the people's dependence on government and prolong the fear of what would happen otherwise.

No thanks to this widespread proliferation of fear, concerts will never be the same. Movie theaters will never be the same. Nor will football, baseball, basketball, and other sports.

Large department stores were on the brink of extinction anyway; they'll probably last another two or three years. The big conglomerates based on online orders such as Amazon and Walmart are going to make it because they have thrived during this time.

The fear is so strong that even if the virus totally disappears tomorrow, people will still be afraid and still won't go to work, and now we've given them resources to support their fear-induced laziness. It used to be that if you were afraid of the virus, you wouldn't have enough money to feed your family, so you had to suck it up and go to work. Now Joe Biden says otherwise: stay home no matter what, and the government (i.e., the taxpayers) will take care of you. He wants to make it that if you're afraid to go to work due to covid-19, that fear in itself will get you a weekly government bailout. Just quit work, and you can collect without having to pass Go. Note, too, that just three days into his presidency, Biden said there was nothing we could do about the trajectory of the virus right now.

Remember when we believed as a people that we have nothing to fear but fear itself? Are Americans winning over fear? Not in this country, not right now.

Three

WE ARE THE VIRUS

*Social media are the platform on which
the real virus grows.*

There is another virus you should be aware (and afraid) of.

It is us: you and me. I say "us" rhetorically, not putting the onus on just you and me, literally, but as in "We, the people," people in general, and we get lumped into that because we use social media.

It is us: you and me.

Whether they know it or not, anyone who has at least one social media account is part of this digital virus, which occurs at the intersection of Big Tech Street and Individual Free Speech Boulevard. Or at least it *was* free speech before the likes of Facebook and Twitter started messing around with it, potentially knocking anyone off who didn't toe the line of political correctness—including former president Donald

Trump. You know all about that story, about how Big Tech has bully-pushed itself to the head of the line of corporate media ruling the roost, fueling the cancel culture mob and having an increased influence in how this country is run.

Social media are the platform on which the real virus grows. So social media are both a blessing and a curse. They are a blessing because the likes of Facebook, Twitter, Instagram, and others have over the last fifteen years given us unprecedented, unfettered access to old schoolmates, long-lost friends, and relatives we haven't spoken to in years. That's just for starters. It has also given us touch points with celebrities, where we can leave a comment below a post made by someone famous, and he or she might even respond personally. A friend of mine once left a comment on a thread started by the comedian and political pundit Dennis Miller, and Miller soon shot a personal reply back to him. That made his day—he was being heard! I didn't have the heart to tell him that it was most likely a social media handler who had replied, but you get the point.

The untouchable are now, in fact, touchable! That's the beauty of social media, especially Facebook. It is a wide-open forum, or at least it used to be. Its doors have started to close bit by bit.

All in all, social media's reach is still extraordinarily significant. More than 3 billion people, or approximately 40 percent of the world's population, has access to online social media. Each of us is "spending an average of two hours every day sharing, liking, tweeting and updating on these platforms, according to some reports. That breaks down to around half a million tweets and Snapchat photos shared every minute." That presents plenty of opportunities for nearly half the world to be frequently exposed to this toxic environment. Note that those numbers were reported in a BBC article in January 2018, so we can assume that the extent of the virus is even more widespread, with more users *using*—which certainly sounds like addiction terminology—now in 2021 than there were three years ago.

The curse of social media is manifested in a number of ways. It starts with the instantaneous dissemination of false, misleading, and otherwise harmful information that has the potential to reach more than a billion people within a matter of minutes, even seconds. The only problem is that the only information that is ever deemed any of those things is conservative information. In the present-day world, the curse of social media often involves political commentary. Pick any political topic you want, and anything goes. Heads will roll, combatants will lose sleep. We see them all the time: hurtful exchanges bouncing among posts, comments, and replies that continually make a mockery of what we like to call mass communications. That's before we even get into areas such as mental health, Internet addiction, emotional insecurities, and just plain waste of time. Social media as a curse? Yes, I understand the irony of a social media star turned conservative figure saying this. However, I have seen behind the curtain. I have seen the disease that we all keep spreading with every touch.

As recently as the late 1990s into the early 2000s—just two decades ago—everybody had political beliefs, just as they do today. Back then, the subjects of discussion might include things like what they thought about abortion or lingering "conspiracy" theories about whether Bill Clinton "had sexual relations with that woman," or if the US Supreme Court had been right or wrong in putting a halt to the vote recount (with the attendant "hanging chads" controversy) in Florida. The last declared George W. Bush the victor in a 2000 presidential election that, even compared to the 2020 voting debacle, stands as the most controversial presidential election in US history. Just think: all Al Gore, Jr., had to do was win his home state of Tennessee to beat Bush, and he couldn't even do that. So there.

Until social media came along—starting with Myspace in 2003 and followed soon after by Facebook and others—everybody had thoughts about political issues. Politics are not new. They aren't something that Americans recently brought about to give us something to hate each other over. Politics are life. They have been around since the beginning, and they will be here until the end. The difference is that now *every* US citizen is a Monday-morning politician! Until social media came along, this didn't exist. At least not in a public forum. Some things just weren't discussed in public, not even around the water cooler. Some of it was taboo in public, some stuff just never came up in conversation. It wasn't worth talking about. The only real opportunity people had to discuss such topics back then was during the day at work or at school. The news also wasn't talking *only* about what political candidates or elected officials had for breakfast or had said about someone's mom.

The 24/7 coverage of politics has changed everything! Back then, those things just didn't come up much in conversation, mostly because there wasn't time for it. At best it was one-on-one conversations during watercooler breaks at work or while meeting up in the hallway between classes at school. God forbid that people had heard everything we actually thought or talked about. *Every single person in the country would be canceled.* You heard me. Every single one of you reading this book has thought something, said something, or done something that you probably "shouldn't have," just like people who look down on people with DUIs knowing the only reason they don't have one is that they didn't get caught! We are all guilty of not being perfect, but the world seems to have forgotten that there was only one perfect person, and his name was spelled J-E-S-U-S. But I digress. That would be as far as things went—quick bursts of conversation with no staying power, no record left behind, no online threads providing a transcript that can be added to indefinitely. Nothing like today, right? The personal interactions twenty years ago provided nothing close to comparable to the assorted communications avenues and gadgets we have at our fingertips in 2021. Welcome to our brave new world, one that Aldous Huxley probably never fully envisioned (and I use the term "brave" here lightly—bravery and social media interaction have little to do with each other). In fact, 99 percent of the things written on social media would never be said aloud in real life. Trust me, I know. I have made an entire career saying out loud and in front of the masses what many never would or could say.

I'm thinking back about twenty years ago or so, say back to the late 1990s. Having a conversation about abortion or gender preference, personal things like that, just didn't belong in everyday public conversation. It just wasn't palatable or entertaining or just plain conversational to talk about those things. But in 2021, via social media, those types of topics are an everyday free-for-all. It's my experience, and I'm guessing one that is shared by many people, regardless of political persuasion or brand of faith, that you know, circa 1999, nobody in school or at work would ask another person his or her thoughts on abortion or adultery in the White House. Nobody talked about it because it was just understood you didn't talk about those things at work or in school. Those things rarely came up in conversation, except on those occasions when there were a few whispers about someone unmarried getting pregnant, or suddenly leaving. "Hey, we're here at work or school, disappearing for a few weeks or a couple months, then coming back with little reason given or offered for their absence." To be fair, I don't believe most people care about those personal issues to this day. Not even the "woke" cancel mobs who claim they care. They just go there because they crave clicks and social media fame for five minutes, so they make a big deal out of nothing. Like what the gender of a potato toy should be.

Everything changed with social media. It makes us shout from the rooftops things we otherwise wouldn't even whisper around others. It, and everything changed. They gave everybody a voice to put out whatever it is they want to say whenever they want to say it. Now, with the click of a button, you can see everything that you either want to know or you don't want to know about a person. The manner in which we hire people for jobs is very different from what it was just a few years ago. When we get a résumé, what's the first thing we do? We look the candidate up on the Internet. The problem is—and I am not immune to this, and neither is anyone, conservative or liberal, who is reading this book—is that we all do it. There is somebody who wants to be in our small social group, or there is somebody who wants to work for our business, and we find out that they believe the exact opposite of everything we believe, politically. Naturally, we go, "That's not going to work."

We would like to pretend that we are above following selfish stereotypes or giving preferential treatment shown to those who agree with us. But the truth is, we're not above that. Everybody has preferences. I would rather that my daughter marry a certain kind of a person, or I would rather that my children do *this* as opposed to *that* (whatever *this* and *that* may be). I like trucks as opposed to sports cars. I like *this* over *that*. We all have preferences. But now, because of our becoming the virus that feeds, and is fed by, interactions on social media, our preferences are branded as racism or bigotry, even though they're not actually racism.

My business partner is an African American. He is a very wise man. He said, "People can say whatever they want about me, but that's not racism. Nor is racism somebody saying hurtful things to you." I agree with him. This is America, after all, and we have freedom of speech. Many Americans exercise the right to tell me what they think of me and where they think I should go on a daily basis. He went on to say, "Racism, however, is when somebody is in a position of power and they use that power against you based on your skin color. Say you own a business and you won't let me come in there because I'm black; that's racism. But if you own a business, let me come in there, let me buy a sandwich from you, then I walk out and you call me the N-word after I'm gone, that's not racism. It's not good, in fact, it's terrible, but that's not racism. You still let me come in there, and I was able to buy my sandwich without you causing me any problems. Then I left—no problem." Again, I agree. The words of the ignorant only if you let them. The even greater truth is that people have the right to be ignorant and be set in their ways right or wrong. This is the American dream: you leave me alone to live my life, and I will leave you alone to live yours.

It's the same thing as a store owner who sees somebody walk in that he doesn't know. He notices that the person has tattoos and piercings all over his face, and he thinks to himself, *Oh, he must be into some weird stuff!* When for all you know, he could be a doctor. One of my favorite viral posts online is of a guy who's got tattoos from the neck down, all the way down his body. He's wearing a tight tank top and is a super-'roided-out-looking kind of guy, and you wonder, *What does this guy do for a living?* Then you see that he's a doctor, and when he has his white coat on, and you can't see all that other stuff. Our looks don't matter; our character does. Our thoughts honestly don't matter, either. Because thoughts without actions are nothing at all.

Social media have enabled us to become our own virus. We have become our own form of disintegrating acid. What we have done to get to this point is that we have decided to no longer keep believing and thinking what we have kept within ourselves our whole life, which, to be blunt, we shouldn't have kept locked away in the first place. We're letting it all out, getting it off our chests. This has happened because, thanks to social media, we are being exposed to diverse cultures and ways of thinking 24/7 from not only across America but around the entire world. We have allowed our core beliefs and perspectives to be bombarded and influenced by an infinite number of outside influences, many radically different from what we had carried around our entire lives.

We now have married couples who are divided over politics. This is true all over. It's just one sign of how our society has changed over the last several decades. Thirty years ago, the likelihood of somebody who was born and raised in Mississippi and now has a job there meeting somebody who was born and raised and working in Chicago were almost nonexistent, save for a small number of folks who might have met in college. Even then, at least one of them had to go well out of his or her way to go to that college or university. It wasn't so long ago that you dated within your community, got married within your community, and that was all you knew—in the vast majority of cases (there have always been exceptions, granted). So most of the time, you and your new spouse probably believed most of the same things and thought the same way.

But the world is smaller now. It's as though somebody has balled up an XXL cotton T-shirt, thrown it into the washing machine, and put it through the dryer, and it has come out the size of a handkerchief. That's what our world has become because of the Internet and social media. We have dating apps where you can find—from right here in South Carolina—a woman in Oregon you think is attractive. You start chatting or messaging with each other, and then in some cases one of you takes a leap of faith and flies to go meet the other. Cheap flights help with that, too. Next thing you know, you are married and living together in New York City—two completely different worlds residing in one spot. It happens, like never before. Rare, yes; unheard of, no longer. That's when the lightbulb goes on and you realize, "Oh, my God, we're actually different!"

Dating sites and apps have started to catch up with the political divide that continues to be fed via social media. Some have a line where you can insert into your profile where you stand politically—whether you're liberal, conservative, or something in between. On top of that, when you are creating or updating your profile, you can say whatever you want, touting your own political (or religious) beliefs, making it clear to whomever happens to be looking at your profile that if he or she, for instance, voted for Trump, you can just forget about it and move on to the next person who pops up in your search. This stuff can get pretty poisonous if you take it to heart, especially if you get into a debate with the other person via a messaging app, even when you know you're fighting a losing cause. It's supposed to be a dating site, after all.

An acquaintance of mine, Mike, got divorced in 2020 after thirty years of marriage. Several months later, he joined a dating site and eventually found a woman who looked and sounded like a perfect match. Mike's preference was a professional woman with an advanced degree, and the woman was all that and more (an attorney, it turned out). Plus they were just a year or two apart in age. In her profile she described what kind of person she was and what she was looking for in a guy, and everything sounded spot on for Mike. They also shared many of the same interests, and the site even rated them as 97 percent compatible. One problem: she identified herself as liberal and punctuated that by writing on her profile that if you were a Trump voter to not even bother contacting her. Well, Mike did contact her to ask why she was so quick to ditch a prospective suitor based on just that one criterion when so much else synced up. She wrote him back, berating and mocking him for supporting a misogynist, telling Mike she wasn't about to put up with his "mansplaining." And that was the end of that. "Mansplaining" is one of the new buzzwords that a liberal woman hits a conservative guy with to shut him up. It usually works because to argue with it is to bang your head against a cement wall a few times. It's not worth it.

There's an old saying, "All is fair in love and war." I would add a third arena to that: politics. All is fair in love, war, and politics. As Mike found out on the dating site, all three are sometimes rolled up into one package. Social media are not very sociable.

This goes back to us being our own virus. It shouldn't matter, but it does. You have to ask yourself that if you are married to the right person, why are you so far apart in voting for something as monumental as the differences between Donald Trump and Joe Biden? There's no splitting hairs when it comes to choosing between Trump and Biden, just as there wasn't in 2016 with Trump and Hillary Clinton.

In that 2016 election, people were saying "My spouse voted for Trump, and I don't know what to do because I voted for Hillary." Well, my question is, how have we become so destructive to ourselves? The truth is, if you voted for Hillary Clinton and your spouse voted for Donald Trump, you two really have no business being together. That's because if you voted for Trump, that means you're more than likely pro-life, pro-faith, pro-freedom, pro-goodness, pro–border wall, and, not least of all, pro-capitalism. If you voted for Hillary Clinton and/or Joe Biden, you're pro-abortion, pro-socialism, anti-gun, anti–free speech, anti-capitalism, and so forth. I would say, again, that social media have become such a viral infection among Americans that we now find ourselves with spouses whom, honestly, we have no business being around in the first place.

In our unwitting roles as components of this worldwide virus, we are also the victims of collateral damage due to our rampant use of the Internet and, in particular, social media. Jessica Brown, who wrote the BBC article referenced earlier in this chapter, cited research that identified factors such as stress, mood, anxiety, depression, sleep, self-esteem, well-being, relationships, envy, and loneliness as being affected by our attachment to and dependence on social media and what takes place there either at our fingertips or with our eyes. These are the sorts of things we don't need to be trifling with just so we can participate in another round of politically based bashing of one another, day after day after day.

For a 2013 study referenced by Brown, researchers sent out texts five times a day for two weeks asking the seventy-nine study participants how they felt and how much they had been using Facebook in the time since they had last been texted. The cumulative results showed that the more time the participants spent on the site, "the worse they felt later on, and the more their life satisfaction declined over time." Another study, which was done in 2016, focused on depression among 1,700 test subjects, finding that those who used the most social media platforms had three times the risk of experiencing depression and anxiety as the others. Combine all that with the combustibility of political discussion—on or off social media—and you have a recipe for some pretty bad times.

There are no surprises there.

Yes, we are the virus, but there are powers at work in social media that feed into it, that help make us into what we are— our own worst enemy at times. One of the complaints levied against social media in recent years by various "experts" is that the social media companies ("Big Tech") weren't doing enough to police the spread of fake news and misinformation, much of it being created and disseminated by foreign governments looking to dump negative influences into the laps of

Americans. Believe me, the likes of Russia and China can do this without having to collude with anybody; they have plenty of skills, moxie, and technology on their own; they don't need anyone's help.

In October 2019, Forbes ran a story headlined "Does Social Media Make the Political Divide Worse?" and the answer was, of course, yes. For years, social media/Big Tech have shown an inability to inoculate itself from this user-generated virus and yet has probably benefited monetarily from it. "Social media is a contributing factor to the political divide in our country," Dr. Nathaniel Ivers, a Wake Forest University professor in the Department of Counseling, told *Forbes*. "It is hard to know, however, if social media is helping to widen the rift or make salient how deep and broad the divide already is."

Politics on social media has become a breeding ground for dissent, with sources of information often creating "something" out of "nothing," stirring up emotions in users and keeping them engaged, and often enraged, while false and misleading information keeps bouncing around cyberspace, egging users on. Big Tech in the last year or so has made token efforts to root out and eliminate false information posted online, but the attempts at solutions have probably exacerbated the problems more than they have helped quell the angry divide.

"With social media, individuals with particular political persuasions seem to 'follow' or 'friend' individuals on social media who share similar viewpoints," Ivers continued. "The difference, however, is that many social media platforms do not appear to filter content based on the accuracy of the

information. Therefore, individuals, groups, and even foreign governments can propagate ideas and information; even
when such ideas have little to no basis in reality. It seems to
me that the goal of those disseminating political information
on social media and through some news outlets has devolved
into how much they can make the other side seem inconsis-
tent, disingenuous, or absurd, rather than to provide accurate
details about events."

Based on my own experiences and observations, we have
become so disdainful, so loathing, and so self-projecting of
our own issues, wants, and desires onto other people that we
forget that other people aren't ourselves. I have friends whom
I've been friends with my entire life. I haven't changed in that
time; I'm the same person. I believe the same things I believed
when I was eighteen years old. But now that I'm in my thirties
and my friends are in their thirties, all of a sudden they want
nothing to do with me because they now see me as a horrible person. But I'm not a horrible person; I'm a patriot, I'm a
veteran, and I'm a family man with a wife and kids whom I
love, committed to being one with my wife in how we raise
our children.

I've always felt the way I feel about things right now. I have
the same love of country, the same Christian beliefs, the same
values when it comes to things like politics and family. Enter
social media and the friends with whom we've reconnected
on there. Okay, stick with me on this sentence, reading it
slowly, because it can be tricky to keep track of: we have contributed to this widespread, voluntarily engineered virus of
which we are a part by letting everybody know what we think

(mostly via social media) and by letting everybody know what we think about what they think, and then they let us know what they think about what we think, and then we hate them for hating whatever it is about us that they hate, and then they hate that about us and what we do. And so on and so forth. We end up with a toxic cycle that we have put ourselves into. It is like a viral infection. Instead of injecting antibodies into ourselves (which would involve removing ourselves from the situation), we just keep walking back in and allowing people to sneeze on our face every day. In so doing, we go right back into social media, and we continue to spread the virus.

I am able to sleep at night because I do not read what others say about me regarding how I express what I think. That makes me an oddity. I don't care what people think. I don't. This is what I believe; either you agree with me, or you don't. I'm not going to fight with you. And I'm not going to hate you if you don't agree with me.

This is how I'm raising my kids. This is what I think. I'm about to turn thirty-four years old as I write this, and I'm sticking with my convictions. Back in the day, it was just understood. "Well, the Johnsons down the road do such-and-such, but we don't do that in our home. This is what we do at our house; the Johnsons can do whatever they want to do. But if you marry a Johnson someday, then you can do what the Johnsons do. But right now you're an Allen, so we do things our way here in this house." In today's world such a viewpoint would be regarded as misogynistic, racist, sexist, and what-not. That is, you can take the beliefs of thirty years ago and now stick them on Facebook for the rest of the world to see and read, and suddenly they take on a new life of their own. You leave yourself open to attack, abuse, and other derogatory remarks.

Politicians are as guilty as the rest of us who make up the virus, often taking to Twitter—Trump was a pioneer in that regard—where they throw out brief "soundbytes," as Ivers calls them, garnering more attention in short bursts than they would by posting lengthy, reasoned political arguments (as in the old days). They provide the bytes, and the rest of us, seeing them, gobble them up, with nothing much good to come out of that.

"[Social media] platforms are ideal catalysts for disseminating soundbytes," Ivers said, "which give [politicians] greater power and influence. With gifs, emotionally stimulating pictures can be associated with these brief messages to accentuate their influence. Statements made on Twitter or other social media platforms are intended to trigger emotions; they are not meant to inform or persuade individuals based on sound reason. In that way, yes, brief statements do contribute to the political divide because I believe the divide is driven more by emotions than it is concepts."

★ ★ ★

The biggest symptom of this virus is that we can no longer agree to disagree. Instead, we have to win. (I'm not speaking for myself but saying this as representative of the general sentiment expressed on social media.) We have to be right. And if we're not right, and if you don't conform to our side of thinking, well, now we are enemies. Now we are fighting against each other, and now you must be destroyed because you're wrong. *You're wrong. You're wrong. You're wrong. And until you're right—when right is not actually being right, it's just thinking the same thing I think that's right.* We have tainted the truth, and there is only one truth. There are not multiple truths. There are not "your truths."

Politics is the biggest facilitator of this. It's like an incubator for germs. We get so intensely—better yet, obsessively—wrapped around politics that we use them as a means of dividing ourselves. We don't even need the government to do it. We divide ourselves because we are the virus. The virus is us. And we need to figure out a way to attack the virus. It starts with ourselves. As I mentioned earlier in the book, you've got to watch the revolution speech in the movie *V for Vendetta.* If we want to know how we got to where we are, if we want to know why we are in the predicament that we're in, we can cast the blame on other people. We can cast it on Democrats; we can cast it on Republicans; we can cast it on the government; or we can cast it on the president or the church or this or that. The truth is, all we have to do is look in the mirror, and there's the problem.

My good friend Andy Frisella once said, "So many people want to be in control." I'll add that this is another part of the virus: the symptom of wanting to be in control of things other than ourselves. First and foremost, though, we need to be in control of ourselves. You want to know if you're in control? Look in the mirror. Andy also said, "If you look in the mirror, and you don't like what you see; if you're fat, overweight, obese, all this other stuff outside of a medical condition and all this stuff, are you in control? No. If you're not in control of yourself, how in the world can you look at other people and tell them that what they're doing is wrong when you don't even have control over the most basic thing that there is— yourself.?"

Part Two

THE DIVIDE

DIVISION IS A GOOD THING?

How do you divide a nation? You convince its citizens that division is a bad thing.

America has always been divided. That is nothing new. We were divided when we founded America; we've been divided since we've been America; we are divided now. The problem is that in today's world, we have convinced ourselves that division is a bad thing. We think of it as a cancer, something that is tearing us apart, when, in fact, we've been divided from the very beginning. What we see now and regard as a disaster of division is old news.

America is an imperfect perfection, if you will. Nothing is perfect, but it can be pretty close. And America is just about as close as you're ever going to get. It is our differences that make us strong. As we are different, we will be divided on many things. But for some reason, in 2021, or this current generation, the society in which we live today, we view division as a bad thing. Let's instead see it as an ability to grow and expand, coming together as different people connected under one flag, as Americans.

Healing can't occur until we're able to have real discussions, real civil disagreements, real civil discourse.

Let's agree to disagree and move forward.

Go with me here. Take your five closest friends out to lunch or dinner (but go easy on your wallet and make it Dutch all the way around). These are the people you love, your BFFs, your everything, they are your world. Go sit at a table, have dinner, have drinks, have a good time. Talk about your sports teams, talk about your girlfriend, your boyfriend, or whomever or whatever it is that you're dating. People are dating trees these days, so talk about whatever it is gets all of you talking, and have the best time ever.

Once things get warmed up (and maybe lubed up), ask them how to solve the national debt, how to solve world hunger, how to end human trafficking, or how to fix racial tensions within the country. Make the question interesting and something for which there will likely be a diversity of opinions and views. Diversity—that word alone should stimulate plenty of fascinating give-and-take conversation.

Be honest with yourself. How's the conversation actually going to go? Are you all going to agree 100 percent on how we should halt child sex trafficking? Are you going to agree 100 percent on whether true racism is still at play within America? Are you going to agree that life starts at conception or life starts after a baby passes through the vaginal canal? Ask yourself an honest question: Are you and your friends really united, or are you actually more divided than you thought?

The answer is very simple. Of course, you will be divided. Of course you will not agree 100 percent, because the idea that two people can agree 100 percent on anything is absolute insanity. We are individual beings, we are individual people. We all have bits and pieces of our lives and circumstances and where we've come from, where we've been, where we're going, and what we're going to do in our lives. We're all different; everyone is going to be different. Even people who grew up on the same street and went to the same school have different experiences that make them different people. Therefore, they are not going to see everything the same way all the time.

There is strength in division of thought, there is strength in division of reasoning, there is strength in division of how we process information, almost like checks and balances being at work. We need to be able to disagree, we need to be able to have civil discourse among ourselves, we need to understand that just because we're united as Americans does not mean that we're going to be united on everything else. And that's okay.

A free America has its roots in a ragtag, redneck militia in the 1700s that grew together and decided to formulate something that was bigger than itself. We had a conversation on the podcast earlier this year when we talked about one of the reasons we've become divided in our country: we have eliminated what we like to call *social norms*. Whereas once a traditional, or "acceptable," family was considered to be male husband, female wife, and their biological offspring all living under one roof, now we have all kinds of variations of families that no one dare call abnormal. It could be a never-married woman raising children born of different fathers; a single man with adopted multiracial children; married or unmarried gay couples with or without children, and so on. That's before we even get into identifying "trans" couples (or people having more than two spouses) and/or children living in any one of a dozen combinations. Then there are women who choose to forgo a professional career to stay home with the kid(s) until the nest is empty. Whereas once this was considered the norm, even noble, now such a living arrangement is looked upon as outdated, even weird, and maybe even a source of suspicion or mockery. One thing should never change: if a woman doesn't want to stay home with the kids, of course she should be allowed to go to work and earn pay equal to that of her male cohorts. She should be allowed to pursue whatever career she wants to do. Likewise, a woman's choice to stay home shouldn't automatically be assumed to be a copout or even a misogynistic approach to oppression, as many enlightened "progressives" would call it. How is being a stay-at-home mom holding a woman down? Know this: many people still believe that protecting the nuclear family is far and away the most important aspect of American society and culture. Liberals insist on a woman's right to be pro-choice when it comes to her pregnancy; why can't she be allowed to be pro-choice when it comes to career versus staying at home?

Then there's the juggernaut known as cancel culture, and now, of all people, it has gone after Dr. Seuss. Am I serious?

Yes, it's true. Six of the books authored by Theodor Seuss Geisel (aka Dr. Seuss) will no longer be published, reportedly because of the books' allegedly racial overtones and insensitivity. Granted, it was the publisher and not a cancel culture mob that pulled back its "cancel culture," using alternative PC terms or phrases such as "It's a moral issue" or "It's a product recall"—they apparently forgot to mention "progressivism"—to describe the rationale for throwing out the six Seuss books, but we all know the dirty little secret. It wasn't just "a moral issue" or "product recall" that inspired Hitler's notorious bonfires. Sooner or later the cancel culture mob—or we could also call it "woke" activists, would have come knocking at the publisher's door, brandishing pitchforks and lit torches. Recalling *Zoo* is no different from recalling and replacing defective airbag deployment devices on a certain make of vehicle. Geisel's crime of having been born in 1904 and brought up in the 1910s and 1920s, a long-ago era during which he was subjected to common cultural influences deemed destructive to society a hundred years later (and thirty years after Geisel's death), has finally come to light. The books *had* to go, figuratively tossed onto one of Hitler's burning piles of books.

Why is this sort of thing happening now? It's because we have decided that certain things now mean different things and those certain things aren't funny anymore. They are harmful, or so we have been informed. Why is it that we're now allowed to cancel things, such as culture? Why is it that we're now allowed to get rid of everything? Division is not the problem in America; cancel culture is. To be able to ruin someone's life, to be able to change things because someone is offended or enough people are offended about things, is the enactment of a very dangerous mindset. Because it's not the majority of people who are offended. Here's the truth.

Most people couldn't care less about your feelings or anything else, and they understand that you couldn't care less about their feelings, either. That's part of being actual adults, with a sense of understanding. There's a sense of "I don't give a crap if you agree with me or not. I don't give a crap if you care if I live or die. I don't care if you hope every single day that I fail financially and desolate on the street. That's because in my daily life, you affect me zero in any kind of way, shape, form, or fashion." For some reason, though, in 2021, people who live thousands of miles away—and will never see the other person—become so offended at what someone says on the Internet that they are affected and feel led to stir up enough controversy to ruin that person simply because he or she said something that they do not like. We have made division a bad thing.

It doesn't have to be that way.

Let's take a deeper dive on this. We're even divided when it comes to Hollywood, and we talked about this on one of my episodes earlier this year. The singer/actress Demi Lovato made the claim that gender-reveal parties are transphobic. So just like that, we can't even agree on what a gender-reveal party is. I know, spare me, right? A gender-reveal party was originally a gathering in which a group of women friends got together to celebrate the birth or upcoming birth of one of the women's new child. Then eventually it was thought that men should start attending the events, so now they do. But as we all know, these sorts of events are miserable for men, so the party organizers started adding alcohol and other drinks, explosions, and cake cuttings and using bows and arrows or play guns to shoot at balloons. This was to give men something of interest to occupy their time while awaiting the verdict on the baby's gender. And it turned into a great time for people as they blew up stuff and popped balloons so powder exploded out. Welcome to the twenty-first century. Thirty or forty years ago, you found out the gender of the child by the name the child was given at birth, because we used to not name our children ridiculous names such as Ice, Water, and XY3.74 to the power.

The most ironic thing about division in America is that we are so blessed, we now have so much in our possession or at our disposal, that we actually have to find things to be oppressed and offended by. We have to look for them and find them, or else we invent them. Ten years ago, nobody was offended by a gender-reveal party. Who cares? Who is actually being offended? This is the biggest question. Why would someone be offended by a gender-reveal party?

Lovato sent out a tweet based on information she had gotten from Not-Binary.org, a coalition of twenty-six hundred scientists, saying that gender-reveal parties are transphobic and gender and genitalia are not the same thing. Two thousand six hundred scientists supposedly back this up. So this is the kind of hard work that thousands of scientists are doing these days, huh? Well, my first thought is that I'm pretty sure that there are a lot more than twenty-six hundred scientists in the world—not much of a consensus from the scientific community here.

By my count, that's not a whole lot of scientists who agree with Demi's harebrained concept that genitals and gender aren't the same thing. This is what she said: "Gender reveals require not just the invalidation of transness, but the impossibility of transness." Let's read it again, those exact words representing the thought process that goes into postulating that gender-reveal parties are transphobic: "Gender reveals require not just the invalidation of transness, but the impossibility of transness." Very interesting. In case you were wondering, transness refers to transgenderism.

This is very, very, very specific, the wording of this. Just like Demi, we're finding things to be divided about, things to be upset about, things to be offended by. The question in this instance is, who's actually being offended by this gender-reveal stuff? The child? It's not even there yet—it's still cooking in the mother's womb. Yes, the child is physically there, but it is not cognizant, and it is not out of the vaginal canal yet. Even if he or she were out of the womb, he or she wouldn't have any clue as to what's going on regarding its gender for a number of years.

I'll tell you who is offended by this. It is people who are not comfortable with themselves, people who are miserable, people who have been diagnosed with hormonal imbalances, people who reside among society's unhappiest folks, people who contribute to the highest divorce rates in the country— these are miserable people who would be upset about a gender-reveal party. And they thank their lucky stars for celebrities such as Demi Lovato, who handed them a silver platter with one more stupid excuse to be offended.

So here's the thing, and let's repeat Demi's unbounded brilliance one more time: "Gender reveals require not just the invalidation of transness, but the impossibility of transness." By that very sentence and that very definition, is she saying that being trans or LGBTQ, in general, is a choice? Because that's what that sounds like if you ask me. Uh-oh, Lovato's membership in the Church of Liberalism is in danger of being revoked. Think about it: if gender reveals require not just the invalidation of transness but also the impossibility of transness, that suggests that being trans and being transgender are something that can be learned, something that can be groomed. It suggests that being trans/transgender can be forced upon a young child.

Why would you be concerned about the invalidation or the impossibility of transness if transgender and LGBTQ are something that is inherent at birth? I'm not saying it is or it isn't; that isn't my job. I know what I believe personally. I am simply repeating what the liberal outcry and the cancel culture mob is saying about the gender-reveal stance taken by Lovato—that it is counterintuitive to their overall point of promoting LGBTQ as part of man's nature and not his nurture. What they're saying is that gender-reveal parties are transphobic because the child is going to be gay and the parties are transphobic, and how dare you? By having a gender-reveal party, you are making it impossible for that child to learn to become transgender.

I am very pro-mind your own business as long as it doesn't affect me and mine. If you want to be a man and claim you're a woman, which as I see as inaccurate—you can't have it both ways—but hey, if you want to live that way, go for it. But if you want me to accept that and you want me to call you a woman's name when you are, in fact, a man, I'm not going to do that. If you want to tell me that the real God is the tree god and that you go out once a week to worship a tree, that's great. But if you expect me to accept that and go outside and worship the tree with you, well, I'm not going to do it.

It used to be that we could all have our own opinions; we could all have our own way of doing things and going about things. And it was just something like, hey, you know what? It's not my way, but if they want to do that, fine. Just, you know, whatever.

But now it's turned into this: Internet articles saying that if you are on a dating site and you are not open to dating a transgender person, you're transphobic.

Call me old-fashioned, but I like my women to be real women (note: I'm every bit a one-woman man). But now we have entered into a twilight zone where what I and others like me believe is not what America was ever supposed to be. America was never supposed to be this thing where we all just agreed on everything. We agree on one thing, that we are all Americans, and that's it. It goes with what I've said about the family unit. My kids argue and fight every single day. Every day it is something, all day. Every day they are bickering and arguing all the time. But let one person who is not in our family say something about one of them to one of them, and watch how quickly they are told where they can go. America was supposed to be the same way, where in a crunch we all had one another's backs. Not anymore. Not even close.

★ ★ ★

Since I'm already making people mad, while we're on this subject, let's just go ahead and take it home, get it across the finish line. Every single bit of this is nothing more than the perversion and sexualization of children, 100 percent. I don't care if it's a gay kid, I don't care if it's a straight kid. Those words written by Lovato—and presumably endorsed by many liberals—attached to children are wrong. It's child exploitation. It's pedophilia. It is the worst of sexual deviation that you can possibly have. Children do not know what sex is. Let's get to the bottom of this, too: whether you're LGBTQ, you're straight, you're transgender, whatever, it all boils down to sex. That's what it boils down to, that's what it's all about. Whom do you want to have sex with, and what do you identify as the person having sex with? Why don't we just change gender-reveal parties to "Who is my kid going to bang thirty years down the road?" Because that's what this is all about.

We are people. We are a species. Everything we do when it comes to relationships revolves around the end result of having sex. It goes like this: I find a person attractive. By finding her attractive, even from a Christian standpoint, I want to date her, I want to court her, I want to engage her, I want to marry her so I can have sex with her. This is the truth. This is simply the way it is. "Be fruitful and multiply," as the Bible says.

Why do we care so much about children being able to decide their gender? Why do we care so much about gender-reveal parties being transphobic? It's because it's a means of trying to sexualize our children. Children don't care about this kind of stuff. Children believe in Batman and want to watch princess movies on the Disney Channel. They don't care about what their gender is or what their sexuality is; these are among the perversions adults pushed upon children. This is going to get us into a lot of trouble.

If you ask an eight-year-old with whom he or she wants to have sex with, he or she is going to look at you like you're insane. He or she has no idea what you are talking about. None. Go ahead, ask your eight-year-old, "Whom do you want to have sex with?" If you're brave enough (or stupid enough) to be that crude and grotesque with your child, which most of these people probably are, go ahead, ask him or her. I can only imagine the looks that you will receive from your child, who has no idea what you, as an adult, are talking about. Nice job, parent.

And so we want to talk about division. Pro-life, pro-choice, division; it's been there forever, for at least as long as I can remember. One side is right, one side is wrong; it depends on whom you ask. Some people say they don't care; others say they care very strongly about one side. I believe that life begins at conception. On the subject of abortion, horrible things happen to good people. They just do: rape, incest, and other bad things. These are terrible things that make up less than 1 percent of all abortion cases. That means more than 99 percent of abortion cases are related to reasons that have nothing to do with rape or incest—things like convenience and wanting to have one's life not "dragged down" by having to take care of a child they don't want. Lust and sex without any responsibility.

This isn't an American issue, it is a world issue. Americans think the world revolves around them. The poorest American is still in the top 1 percent of wealth if you look at the entire world, right? Go to South Africa, and then tell me how bad your life is. Truly, go to South Africa, where you're persecuted for being gay or being a Christian and your genitals or head is chopped off, and then tell me how bad your life actually is here, okay? Life is all about perspective. No matter how poor you think you are, trust me, if you're an American you're not poor, not really. Now, that's a hard pill for a lot of people to swallow, because you might be on the verge of losing your home or you might be homeless. But even on your worst homeless day, you make more money standing at the side of the street asking for money than somebody does working eighteen-hour shifts in a mine in Sudan or wherever the crap it is. Perspective is everything.

Division—or divisiveness—in our country is something that's been here forever.

Let's get back to the subject of pro-life versus pro-choice. I believe that life starts at conception, because, for one thing, you cannot prove to me beyond a shadow of a doubt that it doesn't. And if you can't prove to me beyond a shadow of a doubt that it doesn't, why would you even want to take the chance that you're wrong? What about rape? What about this? What about that? Show me two sonograms, and tell me which one's the rape baby. You can't do it. So you can't tell me that one of those babies matters and the other one doesn't. Also, you can't tell me that the life inside that womb matters so much that you are invading upon its ability to become transgender if its wants to. But if that baby is going to turn out to be a white straight male, you can kill it up until birth and maybe even fifteen minutes after, if you ask Ralph Northam, Virginia's governor since 2018.

These are the stereotypes, and these are the divisive things we have created among ourselves because we have come to believe that division is wrong, division is bad, differences of ideals are something that needs to be extinguished. We can't believe different things. We can't think different ways. This is not from a Christian perspective, obviously. From a Christian perspective, I believe in God first, spouse second, kids next; everything else comes after that, right?

If you ask me, I believe 100 percent that homosexuality is wrong from a religious standpoint. If you ask me point-blank from a Christian perspective what I think about abortion, I'm going to tell you that life starts at conception, in the womb. God doesn't make mistakes. He just doesn't. Well, you then ask, why do horrible things happen to good people? Well, we are so finite in our thinking as people that we don't realize that our life here on Earth is like, God, man, a blip on the radar. It doesn't even matter in the grand scheme of things when you're talking about your life of eternity, right? If you had to ask yourself, would you rather be tortured for eighty years or tortured for all of eternity, which one are you going to pick? I'll pick the eighty years, of course.

Picking the eighty years is a very Christian worldview, one that I embrace. I do not vote Democrat because Democrats do not sit at the most core basis of what I believe. God should be in everything; life begins in the womb. Democrats stray so far from that that there is no way I could ever vote for them. Am I saying that Democrats need to be canceled because they are pro-choice? No, I'm not. I don't believe in cancel culture, no matter how much I disagree with people, no matter how crazy I think they might be, no matter how stupid I think they might be. There are people who are a legitimate waste of molecules and the air they occupy. I truly believe that. If we're being honest.

Am I aware of the fact that my taxes are going to pay for lazy, good-for-nothing people who honestly don't deserve a job? That's because they're probably not going to do a good job, they're probably going to be late, they're probably going to screw things up, and they're probably going to steal. They're deadweight, but Dems love 'em just the same, not because they're God's people, too, but because of PC political considerations and because they can lock up their votes with some well-aimed government entitlements.

Daniel Tosh, who hosted *Tosh.0*, is one of my favorite comedians. One time he was talking about the unemployment rate, and he was actually shocked that the unemployment rate is not *higher*. Because if we're being honest with ourselves, there are a lot of people who should not have jobs because they are horrible people who can just barely blink and walk at the same time. This is not saying that I do not love those people, this is not saying that I do not want what's best for these people. This is just the truth.

"Graham, how can you be pro-life but also pro-death penalty?" Well, that's supersimple. I'll tell you why. Babies are innocent; they have no ability to make any decisions for themselves at all. They are the only people in the world who are blameless for anything. We have laws in this country, we have laws in this world, we have regulations that people are expected to follow. And if you take lives away from people or you do horrible things, sorry, there are just some people who deserve a bullet. That's just the way it is. This is the real world. This is a big-boy, big-girl pants book that you're reading here. That's the truth.

Five

THE PROBLEM ISN'T AMERICA, IT'S YOU

America's being divided doesn't mean that there is
something wrong with America.

S o how do you divide America? You divide America by making Americans think that something is wrong with it. It's like in the movie *Inception*, with Leonardo DiCaprio. In the movie, DiCaprio and his dream-invading team have three layers they need to get to in a person's dream state. The third layer is the most basic, core-principle belief that they have to get to in order to change what needs to be changed to accomplish their mission and make right what is wrong. (See the movie—it would take too long to explain it properly here.) The analogy here in real life is that the most basic thing at our core that we have changed is the widely held belief that there is something wrong with America *because we are divided*. It is a premise with which I staunchly disagree.

We've always been divided, and we will always be divided. It is those divisions that have actually led to the growth and positive change of America. If America were united and everybody believed things today just as they did in 1776, women would still be permanently housebound domestics, barefoot and pregnant, and not allowed to vote. We would still have slavery; we would still believe in bloodletting and other outdated medical practices; and there would be nothing close to the advances we have since made in science and technology. Is that what anyone wants?

Divisiveness has been at the root of all progress—which is not to be confused with the use of the word *progress* that has been hijacked by the diabolical Democrats. But by believing the lie that division is bad, Americans are more divided than we've ever been. That's because we're more divided on the idea of what America is supposed to be than on any other issue or principle. It's not that we, the people, are more divided—we've disliked one another since the beginning—it's just that we are divided on an issue that supersedes all other issues: the state of the nation itself.

You know as well as I do that there are people in your family you can't stand. The sheer mention of them coming to the family reunion makes you not want to go. So don't tell me that you love every other American, because that is simply not true. You want to be an American; you want to be left alone to live your life the way you're supposed to live it under the rules and laws and authority and rights and privileges that we all have as Americans. There is nothing wrong with America. There is, however, something wrong with you.

It's acceptable for us to be divided on topics related to things like social acceptance, social norms, and cultural prosperity or whatever it is. It's okay for us to be divided on these things because we're never *not* going to be. Are we really more divided than we've ever been? I'm pretty sure we had a civil war a while back, roughly 160 years ago, and I'm pretty sure that a lot of people died in it. Are we *really* more divided than we've ever been?

Don't tell me that we have always gotten along or that we have always agreed on everything. No. We came to a decision that we would agree on one thing, that we are Americans. Underneath that tent of being Americans, there is no such thing as "Well, because I'm an American and you're an American, you have to accept everything that I think and I feel, and you have to cater to my opinions and my feeling about that." That's not in there. That's not true. That's not the way that it was supposed to be. That's not real.

We have to get back to knowing that it is okay to believe what you believe and to do what comes naturally to you, even if others might see you as different. Normal is what is normal to you. It is also okay for us to be different from one another but still act in a way that is seen as acceptable to others or normal. Okay. I believe in God. I'm a Christian, but I'm not a Catholic. Yet at the same time, I can walk normally and talk normally. What's inside my head might be different from what others around me are thinking, but I can still walk and talk in a manner that others see as normal: one foot in front of the other, over and over, and speak proper English while able to converse on the same topics others feel comfortable discussing and in that way be seen as normal. That said, I don't go around talking about how messed up I think the Catholic religion is, nor do I talk in such a way as to suggest every Catholic is an enemy and all this and that, and all Catholics are enemies of mine because they don't believe the exact same thing as I do. Same thing with Jewish people. I believe that Jesus was the Son of God, not just a prophet. You know what I mean? But I don't go around telling Jews that unless they believe exactly what I believe, we're now enemies. See what I mean? And that's a whole other bombshell down the road. We've lost the ability to agree to disagree, which is what America was founded on. *Unity* is not in the Constitution. The guarantee of our being united on every issue is not to be found. Where we are united is under principles and ideas. But we're not united on every idea, and we're not united on every principle. We're united under the idea that we are all created equal under God, so we're all entitled to life, liberty, and the pursuit of happiness. We're also united under the idea that if anyone wants to threaten any of that, as Americans we will stand up and fight against it.

Some people are offended by statues. They literally cannot walk past a statue, such as one of Abraham Lincoln or Robert E. Lee, without having a panic attack. Are you sure we're *more* divided and things are as bad as they've *ever* been? Really? I'm speaking to myself here as well. We're not as badly divided as we were at other times in our history, such as during the Civil War. Do we have the ability to get there? Yes, absolutely, but to believe that we're there right now, well, that's not only naive, it's dumb. It is pure ignorance and shows that those who believe such nonsense have no clue as to what they're talking about.

The most divisive thing to ever happen to America was believing that division is a bad thing, that we must be *unified* on all issues and at all costs. Yes, there is a time to be unified across all fronts, as was the case starting on 9/12, 2001. But unity in the legislative process, for instance, and not to be confused with compromise, is a dead end street. There's nothing in the Constitution that says that we're not going to be divided on issues of politics. Good Lord, we have three political parties (Republican, Democrat, and Socialist/Independent), and two of those are majority parties. So naturally we are divided. There's even talk now of a fourth party, which would be absolutely detrimental, and we do not need to go that route.

Even when we decided to declare independence from Great Britain, we were divided. Not everyone wanted to declare independence. The majority ruled, and we went to war, that's all it was; we went to war against the British, not against one another. It was called the Revolutionary War. I say this not to romanticize America, in the process being blinded by patriotism and following leads without question or dissent. I'm the most patriotic person I know, but I'm also a realist. The balance of power is there for a reason.

The majority rules in America, but that doesn't eliminate the possibility of there being division and disagreement along the way. That is the American way. That's the way the military works; that's the way our legal system works; that's the way the police work; and that's how the firefighters work. And so on and so forth. In general, the majority rules in any system based on a hierarchy. We don't have time to deal with less than 1 percent of every issue. Sorry, not that you don't matter, but the US government can't be bogged down in appeasing every single demographic and every detail of every issue all the time. That's not realistic. Nor is it realistic to expect Americans to be bound together on 100 percent of every issue. That's not only fantasy but a sign of a serious problem. That would be scary. The closest we can come to an ideal form of unity in this country is through consensus—majority rule— not unanimity. Somehow we've lost the ability to say "Suck it up" to those comprising a minuscule percentage who stand on a certain side of an issue.

Life does not care what your problems are; not really. In order to be culturally and politically correct, some people will say, "Oh, of course, we care about your feelings, and you deserve to be heard." But the truth is, no one gives a flying crap about your feelings. They give a crap online because it gets them a lot of likes, a lot of comments, and a lot of views. So those people seem to care. But the reality is that people as a whole don't care—the majority of people, anyway.

Are there people who really *do* care? Yes, absolutely. There are many people in America who donate money to charities or causes, such as children with cancer, just like we see in the television commercials for St. Jude Children's Research Hospital. In fact, America is the most generous country in the world, reflective of its Judeo-Christian values. According to the World Giving Index, which is based on ten years of data from annual World Poll surveys conducted in

128 countries between 2009 and 2018 by Gallup, and cited by *U.S. News and World Report*, the United States ranked No. 1 in the world in terms of being most generous. (You might be interested to know that China was nowhere to be seen among the top ten. I know—shocking!) To put a dollar figure next to that, Americans gave $540 billion to charity in 2019 according to the latest Giving USA 2020 report, referenced at nonprofitquarterly.com. Ask China for a loan and see how that goes. "Hey, China, you know, we really need some help, do you think you could donate some money?" See what the people there say, if they say anything at all. I don't know if you have the personal connections to get ahold of, you know, Chinese president Xi Jinping. Ask him for a favor, and see what happens. (Note: Some of you might point out that China already owns more than $1 trillion of our national debt, but that benefits it immensely in return. We're not talking altruism here. Say that to the Chinese leadership, and they'll probably laugh in your face. China wants to keep the value of the US dollar high—holding a chunk of our debt makes that possible—which will keep its exports affordable which helps its economy grow. Trust me, China's ownership of part of the US debt doesn't mean it is doing us any huge favor as an act of self-sacrifice. Its government is much too scheming for that. For what it's worth, as of July 2020, Japan was holding more US debt than China was.)

Americans have even made a sport of divisiveness, with each side of the political aisle accusing the other side's leader of being a particularly divisive leader. Since Barack Obama was president, Republicans and conservatives have accused him of being the most divisive president in history, citing the forty-fourth president's stance and actions regarding racial issues, while Democrats and liberals made similar charges against Obama's immediate successor, number 45, Donald Trump. It's not just a matter of being divisive when it comes to tackling specific issues such as immigration and the border, taxes, and abortion, Americans are now divisive on the subject of divisiveness—who does it worse? Each side accuses the other, relentlessly. It's a no-win proposition.

Yes, there are a lot of people who believe that Obama was the worst president in history, the most divisive president in history, etc. But technology even just five to ten years ago was not what it is now. It's so much more pervasive now, and the bells and whistles of handheld devices have improved significantly in just that short time. So many more people can talk about things now, not just in terms of global numbers but in terms of the percentage of people who are now digitally savvy, especially in using the Internet and more specifically in using social media.

If Obama had been president today, or if he had run and won in 2016 (a brief suspension of reality here; we know a president is limited to two terms) as opposed to Trump, I would say that eventually Obama would have been canceled, as was Trump, and eventually Obama would have been kicked off the Internet for saying, writing, tweeting, or posting something that would have been deemed wholly unsavory and unworthy of being posted on Twitter or Facebook. Such as, for example, if he had tweeted a condemnation and proclamation of guilt of the Minneapolis police officer Derek Chauvin, charged with the murder of George Floyd during jury selection or at the start of the trial). That's assuming Big Tech would be as stringent in applying its standards to Obama's tweet as it was in canceling Trump. An argument could be made that Trump was solely responsible for inciting the US Capitol raid; another argument could be made that what he actually said earlier that day and when and how he said it were misinterpreted and wasn't at all a call to incite but instead a plea to protest peacefully. How you interpret it depends on what side of the political aisle you sit; nothing else. In April 2021 California congresswoman Maxine Waters, a Democrat, specifically called for violence in the streets had Chauvin been found not guilty of murdering Floyd, and no one at Big Tech shut down her dangerous remark. They wouldn't dare. Total hypocrisy.

In the hypothetical Obama 2016 reelection scenario I just described above, Republicans would have raised such a fuss about this or that concerning what he had tweeted or posted, and in this upside-down world, the roles would have been reversed (maybe). Republicans would have made sure the exact same thing was done to Obama (or Hillary, had she won in 2016) as that we saw more recently with Trump. There are a lot of Republicans and conservatives who I don't agree with, so, let's turn the mirror toward ourselves. Plus now that a Democrat is president—Joe Biden, as of this writing—we can assume that a similar cancel culture faces him should he get so bold as to start using social media as part of his communications to the people of this country, although I doubt seriously that Biden would ever have that problem. The guy can barely go two sentences without stumbling while reading a teleprompter. I don't see him tweeting anywhere to the degree that Trump did, and Trump did most of it on his own without a nanny or chaperone around to do it for him.

Allow me to expand a bit on what I just said about not agreeing with all Republicans and conservatives. There's a difference between speaking the truth and looking to antagonize. We have a lot of conservatives right now who've made antagonism their whole shtick: they antagonize, they purposefully make situations worse so they get more likes, more views, more comments, and more followers. They are perpetually stirring the pot to try to make things worse for their own personal gain. This is 100 percent what the Left has done for the past twelve years. That's what they do. Now conservatives are taking pages out of the Left's book for themselves, and maybe that isn't so bad. Give the Dems a taste of their own medicine.

I also believe in fighting with fire. There's a catch-22 to everything, and we have to fight just as aggressively as we're being attacked. That's War 101: you've got to have more firepower, far superior strategies and tactics, and/or a bigger army than the people who are coming at you. No question. You also have to be tactful in what you're trying to achieve. Then there are times we have to realize that maybe we should just shut up and let something go. In such times, close your mouth and let the world spin because, believe it or not, sugarplum fairies don't exist, unicorns aren't real, and the world does not revolve around you. The biggest lie the Devil ever told was that he didn't exist. Well, the biggest lie that America ever told was that division is a horrible thing within our country when, in fact, we've been divided the whole time. We're never going to agree on everything, and that's *good*.

The Founding Fathers wanted us to agree on just a few things. At least get the basics right, right? A little consensus on a few foundational principles goes a long way, except we can't seem to achieve that anymore. We can't even agree that we are all equal in the image of God, that all men have the right to life, liberty, and the pursuit of happiness, that all people are protected by the First Amendment, the Second Amendment, the third, the fourth, the fifth, even though most of you reading this book can't even tell me the first ten amendments, which make up the Bill of Rights. The Founding Fathers knew that we were never going to agree on everything because they were slapping one another in the face in the courtrooms trying to hammer it all out. Regardless of what you think you remember reading in your school history books, those people didn't agree on everything. The only reason that France came to help us was because Benjamin Franklin was part of a sex cult in Great Britain known as the Hellfire Club, and that's how it all started in the first place. But nobody wants to talk about those things except me. According to a History Channel report, as cited on the website of *Philadelphia* magazine, Hellfire was "a fraternity dedicated to drinking, sex, and at times ridiculing Christianity and mocking its sacred rituals. Members met in monastaries [*sic*] to revel in black masses and drunken orgies. An occasional participant was the American Ambassador to Great Britain . . . Benjamin Franklin."

Those were flawed people; they weren't perfect. What they did have was a shared vision and an idea, an idea from which every single one of us has prospered. After that it was just working out the details, arguing over a bunch of points, and reaching a mutually agreeable middle ground. As a result of achieving that world-changing consensus, you now are able to read this book freely and without guilt, even though you might think that this is a privilege that some people in America don't deserve to have. But what *you* think on this particular matter doesn't matter. Our Founding Fathers ruled it was to be so— so live with it (and I hope you are enjoying this book). Guess what? In South Africa, people aren't allowed to read whatever they want to read. In some countries, you can be executed for reading the Bible. Think about that for five seconds.

Everybody wants to make everything political, but everything doesn't have to be political. Politics is life. I agree with that. Some people will say, "I just can't do politics." Well, then, you don't live in reality. Because politics are life, although there are certain things that shouldn't be political, like loving America or loving a daughter or a spouse. We love them for their good qualities, we love them for their bad qualities. It shouldn't be political to love free speech whether it's speech that you agree with or not. In fact, free speech is for everyone, not just people with whom you agree. It shouldn't be political to want to live your life your way. And it shouldn't be political to tell everybody to mind their own business and not expect everybody else to cater to you because that in and of itself is selfishness, it is entitlement, and that is not what America is about.

Those of you who have problems with Christianity and want to go worship your tree or pet salamander or whatever it is that floats your faith, have at it. No problem; not in America, at least. Just realize how privileged and blessed you actually are even to be able to do such crazy things. Go to China and tell the government you want to start a church, or publish a book critical of it, or try to open a business free of state control. Go to parts of Asia, go to parts of Africa, go to parts of Iraq and Iran, tell them that you want to practice Christianity, and watch what happens. Meanwhile, I'm lovin' me some United States of America right now. Care to join me?

This bears repeating, and I'm going to keep pounding it home: we were never supposed to be united on everything, because that's absolutely impossible. I know, tell that to Joe Biden, whose 2021 inauguration address was all about unity. Joe just doesn't get it. We were supposed to push our differences aside and agree on certain core principles as Americans, and that's it. Everything else was open to discussion, debate, and finding a consensus in which not anybody gets everything he or she wants. That was America.

How can you have civil debate, civil discourse, to decide on a direction if everybody agrees? That doesn't do anybody any good. There's no need to talk about anything if we all agree. Besides, that's no fun. The reason we are losing America is not that we're losing the people. The people have already been messed up, divided, ticked off, hating each other for as long as America has been here—and that's okay. Really. We're losing America because we are forgetting what America was supposed to be. It was supposed to be a group of people who are different, who believe different things, who believe certain things, who can disagree politically and religiously but can all agree on certain core principles of being American. The mechanisms fostering such a coming together even with divergent viewpoints are still in place. America is not supposed to be a utopian society where a unicorn farts on you and you're the chosen one. Nobody cares about any of that stuff because it's not real. America is as real as it's ever been, but so many of us have lost sight of that, like ships being lost at sea, and it's always nighttime and no one can see in the dark.

Let me shift gears here, while still staying on point. Let me break this to you bluntly if you have kids in school or college: they're not likely going to make a hundred grand a year straight out of college—and for the sake of perspective, I'm referring to an undergraduate or graduate degree. An MD or DMD, on the other hand, is a different story. Maybe. In fact, most people I know who are rich never even went to college and/or graduated. Okay, now take a seat: we're losing America because we're sending our kids to college. College is a gigantic waste of time and money.

One of the biggest issues with division in our country right now is college campuses, which have become the nation's top purveyors of the absurd. College campuses are breeding grounds of false information, phony ideologies, and greatly misconstrued understandings as to what rights we have as Americans and what America is supposed to be. The left-leaning bias in American colleges is a jaw-dropper when you look at numbers. Wesleyan University president Michael Roth, writing in 2019 on Quora and cited by *Forbes*, said this:

There is no denying the left-leaning political bias on American college campuses. Data show that the professoriate has moved considerably leftward since the late 1980s, especially in the arts and humanities. In New England, where my own university is located, liberal professors outnumber their conservative colleagues by a ratio of 28:1.

How does this bias affect the education we offer? I'd like to think that we left-leaning professors are able to teach the works of conservative thinkers with the same seriousness and attention that we devote to works on our own side of the political spectrum—but do we?"

It's doubtful, although I give props to Roth for disclosing that he is left leaning, which is to say that he's *liberal* and knows it. I'll go a step further than Roth and say that left-wing bias isn't just present at many, if not most, colleges and universities, it is actively involved. It wasn't so long that in some fields, any sort of political partisanship or activism of employees outside of or in conjunction with work was considered a conflict of interest and could even be grounds for termination. Apparently, that sort of workplace philosophy isn't even on the radar in academic circles.

Mitchell Langbert is an associate professor of business at Brooklyn College, which is part of the City University of New York (CUNY). In a commentary he wrote for the James G. Martin Center in October 2020, titled "Who Says Academia Isn't Awash in Liberal Bias?," he told of a Brooklyn College faculty group known as "Rank and File Action" that doesn't hide its inherent political bias. For instance, the group sent out a university-wide invitation promoting an event that was to feature the Marxist Democratic Socialists of America chapter of a nearby community college. "RFA describes itself as 'a group of militant rank & file activists at CUNY challenging the culture of austerity in higher education and demanding a more democratic fighting union,'" he wrote.

When Langbert discussed left-wing bias on college campuses, he wasn't just making sweeping generalizations from afar; he sees plenty of it right where he is. He told of a CUNY Law School student, Rafaella Gunz, who withdrew from school after being relentlessly harassed by left-wing activist students as well as teaching assistants, no less, for opining that Israel has a right to exist. Reportedly, the school's faculty and diversity department didn't offer Gunz any protection from the badgering, either. Here's the kicker: Gunz, according to the *Jerusalem Post*, is self-described as a "liberal, feminist and bisexual woman and activist." But even that wasn't enough to get her a break for a single time of speaking outside the liberal party line.

You want more? Here are two more, among countless others:

- As of October 2020, the University of Central Florida was investigating tenured professor Charles Negy over tweets in which he expressed doubt about the existence of "institutional racism." Reportedly, the university was searching for an excuse to fire Negy, with "misconduct" in his teaching among the pretexts being considered.

- UCLA accounting professor Gordon Klein was temporarily placed on punitive leave for refusing to alter his and the university's policy on final exams after the death of George Floyd. Students had demanded that Klein be fired. Note, though, that although he was reinstated, he was targeted for what was described as "humiliating publicity."

There's not much tolerance or diversity of thought going on at either Central Florida or UCLA. Pitiful.

I am a firm believer in taking a gap year, a year off after graduating from high school before going to college, and putting it to good use. I am a firm believer in getting out and going to work, sweeping the floor, draining the grease out of Sonic when you're working in the back with twelve-hour shifts and being paid minimum wage. I am a firm believer of understanding what life is actually like, not what your professor says it's like—that same professor who is now exempt from the real world because he or she can't be fired once he or she achieves tenure. Professors can do, say, teach, and give out grades whenever and however they want. I don't believe in any of those things.

The sorriest person in the world is the business management degree holder, straight out of college, who thinks he or she knows everything about how to run a business when he or she has never actually run a business. In 2021, who gives a crap what your degree is? This is the world we're in. This is the real truth, right? Who gives a crap? Nobody. Nobody cares because this is a different world that we live in. There are nurses in California who have graduated with a four-year degree, and now they have to work for free for a year before they are deemed experienced enough to be hired by a hospital.

Here's the truth. I believe that college has become extremely overrated. What do I mean by this? Back twenty or thirty years ago, it was all about college. Whoever had the most prestigious college degree was going to get the best job. Now we live in a different world with different meanings and different ways to get things done. The entrepreneur and Internet personality GaryVee (Gary Vaynerchuk) says it best. One of my favorite videos of him is him talking about the educational system in which he says that it's the only system that has not evolved in the past fifty years. Back when I went to school, it was all about memorization: learning equations, learning how something works, learning who George Washington was, being able to define this, define that. Well, nowadays, why do I need to memorize *pi* when all I have to do is grab my cell phone and ask Siri to tell me what the square root of so-and-so is?

Why do I need to memorize anything when there is technology readily available to do it for me? I'm not saying that you don't need to know how to read, write, do basic arithmetic, or summarize the history of the country in which you live. Those are four staples that take maybe six years to master, and then the rest of it is off to the races. What we should be focusing on is what we need to do to hone skills, hone trades, hone the ideas that are going to change the world. Many of the richest people either didn't go to college or never graduated college: Bill Gates, Mark Zuckerberg, and others. They were forced to do something that college graduates think they don't have to do. They think that just because they have that little sheet of paper, they're automatically entitled to a six-figure-a-year job and to respect and dignity in the workplace, when the truth of the matter is that nobody gives a flying crap about your degree, anyway. It's the truth.

Let's go back to the idea of a gap year after high school—I am pro–gap year all the way. It should be mandatory that you can't go to college until you're at least nineteen years old. The second you graduate high school, you have to get an apprenticeship at minimum wage. You should have to scrub the floors, clean toilets, do the worst jobs—and probably three different or four different jobs, one per quarter (changing every three months). You go and you do those apprenticeships, and you learn what it's actually like to work a job. You learn what it's like to work from the bottom up. And *then* you go to college, because now you have some semblance of a clue about what you actually want to do. Those who have no clue and go straight to college anyway end up amassing all sorts of student loan debt, are being handed a next-to-worthless degree at graduation, and now have no idea how to pay off the debt.

All of the systems in place are designed to weaken our society and make us believe that our own feelings matter more than someone else's feelings. Everybody's got feelings. The truth is, most people don't care about yours, and it's always been that way. But somewhere along the line, we convinced ourselves that we used to be united on those things. Not so. That's a lie. Those "good ol' days" don't exist. We used to have slavery, we used to not allow women to vote; it took more than a hundred years for our nation to fix that last part. Are you kidding me? We haven't been divided, you say? What in the world are you talking about?

People will make you believe that the things that we used to be divided on are examples of why America was never great and isn't great now. Don't listen to them. They are cynical crybabies who don't know American history. Again, I would argue that because we were divided on those issues and fought through them, we became a better nation. Those divided ideals were part of our inherent divisiveness, thank God. Divisiveness is what's led us to make the changes needed to forge a positive direction for America.

Divisiveness is not the problem. Believing that Americans are supposed to be united on everything is.

Wise up, America. I'm talking about you, me, all of us. We're in this together, even when we're apart on key issues.

Part Three

THE RUIN

Six

ALL LIVES MATTER

*"People no longer know what racism actually is. They are
confusing personal preference with actual racism."*

Blame Black Lives Matter. I do.

Blame it for in large part giving us the most racially
divided America since the days of segregation more
than fifty years ago.

No doubt BLM proponents who read this will express
their phony outrage and maybe issue a few threats. What better way to promote racial justice and peace among ethnicities,
right? Away from the cameras and social media campaigns
and in their most secret places, however, BLM organizers
will not only agree that I am right but will be proud of it. It
means that their message, however garbled it may be, is getting through and it is being heard.

As suggested by their rhetoric and actions, Black Lives
Matter is following a grand plan to disable America as we

know it—then destroy it. Cancel America from within, as communism tried to do during the 1950s and for the next several decades. And Black Lives Matter then prepared to replace America as we knew it with what exactly? It doesn't matter. Start by defunding and, with any luck, disbanding police forces nationwide. I can't possibly imagine that Dr. Martin Luther King, Jr., would have condoned this nonsense predicated on intimidation and destruction.

For BLM and its antifa allies, the mission is all about anarchy, not assimilation. True peace and understanding among the races, especially black and white, is the last thing BLM wants. It needs racial strife like the rest of us need oxygen, just to survive. Without it, it is defunct. Sunk. Ironically, the May 2020 death of George Floyd at the hands—and bent knee—of a cop threw BLM a life preserver. The cop-induced death of a black man was too good an opportunity to pass up. It gave BLM a booster shot of validation and the cheerleading support of liberal groups to cut swaths of death, destruction, and mayhem through our cities—the majority of which, ironically, were run by liberals. Black Lives Matter doesn't want to just tear at the fabric of America, loosening a few strands of cloth here and there; it wants to rip it apart, knowing that whatever it is that is holding America together is hanging precariously by a thread.

Yes, black lives matter (all lowercase), absolutely. No rational, nonracist human being disagrees with that statement at all. But Black Lives Matter itself? We're talking two different things here, an admirable motto versus the abominable Black Lives Matter, the corporation. Black Lives Matter,

Inc. The phrase "black lives matter" was not meant to be a bad thing; it was meant to empower a community that lives and resides here in America. American citizens of all ethnicities and backgrounds can embrace that motto and take it to heart in how they conduct their lives and treat others. Unfortunately, that's not what this is all about.

Black Lives Matter, Inc., is the problem, and it lacks realistic, reasonable solutions. Black Lives Inc. is involved in Marxist ideology, and its world is not just about black people—it's about anarchists and Socialists bound as one. Check this out for yourself: if you want to donate money to Black Lives Matter, your donation goes through an organization known as ActBlue. To answer your next question, ActBlue is a fundraising organization known to donate to Democratic purposes. According to its website, secure.actblue.com, as of mid-March 2021 ActBlue had raised just under $8.5 billion in political contributions since 2004, boasting a roster of more than 13.7 million Democratic donors whose information is registered with ActBlue. BLM is one of the Democratic Party's pet offsprings, a prodigal son or daughter (or pick whatever other gender identity you wish; plenty to go around). At the bottom of ActBlue's home page, it is written, "Trusted by the Grassroots: Powering Democratic candidates, committees, parties, organizations, and c4s around the country." Swell. Granted, WinRed does the same thing for Republicans and conservatives. But one difference is that you don't see an entity called White Lives Matter using a donation button running through a funding group whose primary mission is to donate to political purposes.

What has happened with Black Lives Matter over the last several years is the same thing that has happened with the #MeToo movement. There is a racial problem in America, no question. In principle, the #MeToo movement, at its most basic, was meant to address a similar issue. Women, of course should speak out when they have been harassed or attacked, and they should be allowed to speak out freely. The accused should be named, and people who have committed such acts should be brought to justice. I believe this *100 percent.*

But something changed at some point in time. It was quick, and it hasn't been good: false accusations and politically motivated lies. Some proponents of the #MeToo movement were unable to resist the chance to exploit it to seek revenge or just hurt somebody, when there really was no cause to do so; classic cases of guilty until proven innocent. That's the problem with society today: things decay and become cancerous very quickly. What started off as a credible way for women to empower other women to come out and speak out about their assaults or their PTSD from unwanted sexual advances turned into a canceling of all men. It turned into an "all men are bad and all men should be taken down" movement. The #MeToo movement turned into an anti-man movement very quickly. We have now seen this with the Black Lives Matter movement, which has become an anti-white movement.

This is a bad time in our nation to be a straight male. Guilty until proven innocent, and maybe the latter doesn't happen. Shameful.

I exposed what's going on with Black Lives Matter and ActBlue about a year ago. That got me fact-checked because there's no way to prove directly all that has happened between ActBlue and BLM, and I seriously doubt they would open their books for me. ActBlue has very specific wording about what it does, including saying that money not specifically allocated toward certain groups or activities can be used at the discretion of ActBlue in any way, shape, or fashion. As I write this, even Black Lives Matter supporters are asking questions: Where is the money? Where did it all go? What is going on? Me! Me! Me! Let me answer that question in part. One possible destination of a sizable chunk of that money has apparently been the coffers of one Patrisse Khan-Cullors, who describes herself as a Marxist leader of Black Lives Matter. It was reported in April 2021 that Cullors had gone on a real estate "spending spree" in which she had bought four "high-end" homes in the United States for a combined $3.2 million.

Who knew that burning down businesses, orchestrating riots, and being an intimidating nuisance could be such a profitable job? One of her homes, which she purchased for $1.4 million, is situated in a tony Los Angeles neighborhood where the vast majority of her neighbors are white. Once Cullors's lavish spending on herself was exposed in the media (a shocking development), the following message was posted on her Instagram page: "This movement began as, and will always remain, a love letter to black people. Three words: Black Lives Matter, serve as a reminder to Black people that we are human and deserve to live vibrant and full lives."

Black Lives Matter, Inc., is a Democratic-controlled super-hub created to divide and destroy our nation, plain and simple. Getting back to what I said earlier, Black Lives Matter,

Inc., and the motto "black lives matter" are two separate things. It's just like understanding the difference between the Left and liberals. They are not the same people. Liberals are not the Left. The Left is not liberals. It is very important to realize what you're talking about when you say these things.

Black Lives Matter's march forward has led to violence and riots in the streets of many cities, providing a breeding ground for terrorist organizations such as antifa to pop up. We talk about civil disobedience within society and civility among citizens. Dr. King spoke about peace in protest. Forget all that. Black Lives Matter, Inc., operates by instigating an utterly cancerous deterioration of those things within our country. You tell me how *civility* and Black Lives Matter belong in the same sentence. What BLM is aiming for is division across multiple platforms. We see this in the fundamental facilitation of a black national anthem and the call to support only black businesses (I suppose that means giving a hand up even to those black-owned businesses that were vandalized, gutted, or destroyed in 2020). Sacrifices have to be made, Buster.

The Biden administration has bought into this racially based mentality to single out companies that are majority owned by black Americans to receive funding assistance. In late February 2021, Biden was set to launch a two-week program under the Paycheck Protection Program (PPP), which is part of the American Rescue Plan Act, to benefit, as CNBC reported it, "smaller, minority-owned firms and sole proprietors left behind in previous rounds of aid." Well, I'm fairly certain there were plenty of smaller firms *not minority owned* that likewise missed out on the coronavirus-related breaks provided during previous rounds of PPP relief. I know this firsthand because the company I co-own, Nine Twelve United, was denied such PPP funding. My Nine Twelve business partner—our ownership is split 50/50—is, in fact, an African American veteran, but we were denied a PPP grant because he is not 51 percent owner of the business, "only" 50 percent.

Biden based his 2021 inauguration address on a call for *unity*. What a crock. Things like PPP favoritism based on race divide our society even further. *All lives matter!* Why that is any more controversial to say than "black lives matter" is beyond me. This is the craziest thing I've heard in my entire life. By saying "all lives matter," you are in fact being more American than anyone who is saying, "black lives matter." Did you know that by saying "black lives matter," you are excluding 76 percent of the population in your statement? I saw multiple videos of people using nutty analogies to promote "black lives matter" and denigrate those who embrace "all lives matter." Freaky stuff, man. Like "Well, you know, your refrigerator is not working in your house, but the house next to you is on fire. So naturally, you deal with the house that's on fire first." I even saw a video gone viral of a girl saying that she's going to stab you, and then while you're bleeding out from being stabbed, she's going to hold up her paper cut and say that her paper cut matters, too.

These are typical of stereotypical lies used to justify attacks against police departments, or at least demand defunding of police. This type of politically charged nonsense is based on false facts not supported by FBI databases. Also, police are more likely to be shot or shot at by African Americans, white Americans, or any Americans than the other way around (African Americans being shot by police). This sort of data do not support what the BLM cause says is actually going on. The facts don't care about your racism because it's normally the people who claim racism first who are actually the ones being racist. Welcome to the world of Black Lives Matter, where wrong is right.

I'm still waiting for an answer: what exactly is wrong with saying "all lives matter"? And what is so bad about our national anthem ("The Star-Spangled Banner")? Why do we need a black national anthem? Or a Hispanic American or Asian American one, for that matter? I am aware that there is a song, "Lift Every Voice and Sing," which has been accepted by the black community. I'm good with that. But it has no place in the same category as the national anthem.

If you have a problem with "The Star-Spangled Banner" as the national anthem, then submit a song to Congress for consideration, and let's vote on it. We have a process for things like that. The problem is that nobody wants to do that anymore. People just want to say things, or at least repeat them enough times, and make them true. Liberals stole the word *progressive* to describe themselves, and they said it a few million times, and I guess that makes it official. They tout themselves as the "progressive" party, even though half the country can make the argument that liberals are anything but progressive. Referring to myself as Brad Pitt a thousand times doesn't make me a movie star.

There is no *truth* anymore. There is "your" truth or whatever truth we're *feeling* at the time. Twenty years from now (I hope), people will look back and ask, "What the crap was that? What is a black national anthem? When do we get to hear the white national anthem?" Within multiple national anthems to cover every major demographic group, pregame rituals would be an hour and a half long. We would have the black national anthem, the regular national anthem, the Asian national anthem, the Hispanic national anthem, the gay national anthem, so on and so forth. What about the Christian national anthem or the Islamic national anthem? Imagine the confusion that would transpire when an Asian American gay person who practices Judaism wins a gold medal. Which anthem will be played and which flag raised at the medal ceremony? Get it wrong, and the International Olympic Committee (IOC) will get its pants sued off by some ACLU lawyer for causing emotional duress. Total freak show.

I considered making a complete list of every conceivable national anthem that could be arranged, scored, and recorded to have on hand as needed for any public event. There's a problem with that, though. I'm afraid I would leave off one or two groups deserving of their own anthem, and that would get my books canceled, just like Dr. Seuss.

The term *national anthem* is there because it includes everyone. Hence the term *national anthem*; hence the phrase "all lives matter." "All lives matter" is, in fact, the only non-racist slogan there is in this context. Do you have another one in mind that fits the bill of being totally inclusive? "Every life matters" or "100 percent of lives matter," perhaps? I think we should just drop all of it and adopt "All lives matter" as an official national slogan because it is the only statement that encompasses everyone equally across the board. Everyone can get behind it, even Joe Biden, as he would now achieve his goal of a nation united.

You want diversity? "All lives matter" fits the bill. But the people who don't like "all lives matter" say it messes things up: "black lives matter" matters only when it can be used for political purposes. That brings us around to someone like David Dorn, who was a seventy-seven-year-old retired police captain in St. Louis at the time of his untimely death—and a black man. On June 2, 2020, Dorn was shot and killed while trying to stop the burglary of a pawnshop—a burglary that took place in the midst, and presumably as part of, a Black Lives Matter "protest" in St. Louis.

Ask a hundred people on the street of any city in America if they know who George Floyd was; then ask them who David Dorn was. In fact, ask the same question of one hundred card-carrying BLM members as well. Any guesses as to which man will come out better known? I'd venture to say the combined score of the two surveyed groups would be about 196–4 in favor of Floyd. Unquestionably. Both men were black, and Dorn is every bit as dead as Floyd is, even though Dorn was neither high on drugs nor handcuffed while trying to resist arrest when he died. If Black Lives Matter said or did anything to honor Dorn after his death, I didn't hear about it. Did you? Yet Floyd has been practically canonized and will probably make it to sainthood one of these days, and they can play the black national anthem at the ceremony. Black Lives

Matter didn't care because it doesn't care about black lives that don't fit its agenda.

All lives matter.

Cancel culture is the true cancer of America. Black Lives Matter is a living, breathing form of cancel culture. Everything about anything that happens now is susceptible to cancel culture, which is far more transmissible than any strain of covid-19. Anti–cancel culture sayings, statements, and beliefs, such as "all lives matter," are now considered wrong, borderline criminal. But cancel culture believers and activists, like Black Lives Matter, are considered commendable. Give them a medal. The only reason that Black Lives Matter is such a high-profile thing is that if you don't believe in that statement but you believe in "all lives matter," you are destined to be canceled.

That is beginning to happen here. We don't have an actual Gestapo force—yet—but we're starting to see that with the cancel culture police and mobs going after people simply for saying "Hey, you know this Black Lives Matter thing is actually divisive. *All* lives matter." Stand on any street corner in any American city and announce that a few times—you don't even need to yell that loud—and watch what happens. If a paddy wagon doesn't arrive soon, some unwanted visitors will.

It goes even farther than that. If you say "all lives matter," that means you can't kill babies in the womb, and now you have the *Roe v. Wade* cult all over your (backside). You see, if all lives matter, then you can't play the victimhood mentality card of "Well, I'm black, and that police officer pulled me over *only* because I'm black." I'm a white guy, and I've been pulled over a bunch for various things, and the only times I've ever gotten a ticket were from a black police officer. Is that racism? How can I get ahold of the ACLU?

If we really cared about people, we would understand that "all lives matter" includes everyone in America equally. That's the whole point. But we don't believe in that anymore. We don't care about everyone. We care about ourselves. That's why Black Lives Matter started in the first place and now flourishes. We shouldn't give special treatment to people based on the color of their skin. We give special treatment to white people, or black people, or Asian people, or Hispanics, solely because of their skin color. We should give equal treatment across the board.

Let's take the subject of race in America to another level. That's when we open up another can of worms using terms like *white supremacy* and *white privilege* to beat up on white people even more. This is where racial considerations really go off the rails. White privilege does not exist. That's evident even in my own little world. Let's address terms such as *white privilege* and *white supremacy* that are used the most, often in referring to police officers and how they conduct the business of law enforcement. I belong to the reserve sheriff's department in my county, and every now and then I go on ride-alongs with them or the police. When I go on these rides, about 90 percent of the people who are arrested or at least questioned or end up going to jail are white. It works this way every time.

What happens is that some people don't put things into the proper context, yet they gripe about alleged racism the loudest. I recently had a conversation with someone who told me that some of their liberal black friends complain repeatedly about how they have been profiled by police officers. So I asked that person, "Where do these friends of yours live? Where do they come from; what communities?"

"Well, you know, they come from the more ghetto areas and places like that."

I said, "Well, there's your answer."

When I said that, I got this weird look back at me, like "What the heck are you talking about?"

"Look, I'm not here to PC people and to placate you," I said. "I don't care what you think about me. I care about the realities of situations."

Put yourself into the shoes of those police officers for one second, the ones who patrol the areas with the highest crime, the highest poverty rates, the least education. What do you think they're going to find there? They're going to find the worst jobs market, the most rampant drug use, and the highest rates of crime. Law enforcement is out in massive force in those areas because they are where most of the biggest problems happen: shootings, stabbings, drugs, rapes. Those cops are on high alert all day every day, knowing that at any moment somebody there might try to kill them. They are sitting ducks and are on edge more than normal. Wouldn't you be? I say to this person, "You don't think about that. You don't think about that for one second. Instead, you point the finger at the wrong people, making the cops the scapegoats for all this."

Here's one truth progressives just can't handle : throughout the entire country, the cities, counties, and states with the highest crime rates, highest poverty levels, worst school systems, and highest drug use are run by Democrats. For example, starting at the top of NeighborhoodScout's 2021 list of the hundred most dangerous cities in America (highest violent crime rates) and going in descending order, the first ten large cities we find are Detroit at no. 1, St. Louis no. 2, Memphis no. 3, Baltimore no. 4, Cleveland no. 16, Kansas City, Missouri, no. 17, Milwaukee no. 23, Oakland, California, no. 26, New Orleans no. 34, and Nashville no. 42. As of May 2021, guess what all ten cities had in common. Yup, Democratic mayors.

What ends up happening is that there is a vicious cycle within the black community in which fathers abandon their wives, girlfriends, and children, and that sets things into motion. Over and over it happens, from one generation to the next. Those aren't my words. They are the words of the likes of Candace Owens, Brandon Tatum, David Harris, Jr., and Larry Elder, all of whom are African Americans who aren't afraid to speak the truth. "Based on the hierarchy of what's impacting minority Americans, if I had to make a list of 100 things, white nationalism would not make the list," said Owens, a black conservative commentator and activist. "I would argue that right now, we have a social environment that is hostile toward men and does not inspire masculinity or being a man and what it means to be a father figure in a household. Black on black crime is a huge issue in America right now, but people don't like to talk about that."

There are public schools in the city of Baltimore in which as of 2019 only 13 percent of fourth graders and 15 percent of eighth graders were reading at a proficient level or better; the respective numbers for math proficiency were 15 percent for fourth graders and 10 percent for eighth graders, and many of those students are African American. The Baltimore City Public Schools website has a demographic breakdown of enrolled students showing that 75.7 percent of the district's total enrollment of about 78,000 students enrolled as of 2021 were African American with 14.2 percent Hispanic/Latino and 7.5 percent white. Yet these poorly performing schools receive ample funding each year because the handing out of dollars is apparently not based on student or school performance. As of 2019, Baltimore City Public Schools ranked third in the nation behind New York City and Boston for per student spending at $16,184 per pupil.

We're not punishing bad teachers because teachers have tenure; they cannot be fired. On top of that, there is the breakdown of the nuclear family. There are fathers who are in and out of jail, abusive to and/or cheating on their spouse. That begets sons growing up without fathers and going to— or at least zoned for—a school in a neighborhood that has high poverty, high crime, low education. What kind of job do you think they're going to get upon graduation? Well, unless they have a solid work ethic and the desire to overcome their circumstances—and some do—they probably are already geared to stay where they are. Plus, they've probably had sex out of wedlock and have either a kid or kids, or one is on the way. They can't make money, so their only choice is to get into the drug culture and along with that the crime culture. And then what ends up happening? They get arrested. Now there is another generation of African American children growing up without a father.

If Black Lives Matter, or black people in general have a gripe about police forces massing in high-crime neighborhoods in cities, they might want to take it up with the man largely responsible for making that happen. He did it via the Violent Crime Control and Law Enforcement Act of 1994; in short, the 1994 Crime Bill. That's the federal legislative act that gave us, among other provisions, mandatory minimum sentencing, mass incarceration, and the controversial "three strikes" mandatory life sentence for repeat violent offenders. Over the last twenty-five-plus years, that bill has been knocked for failing to curtail crime while increasing incarceration rates for black offenders, as outlined at FactCheck. org. It's an albatross around the neck of a lot of men and women who voted it into existence in 1994. Now, here's the real kicker—are you seated, Black Lives Matter members and supporters? The author of the bill who essentially shepherded it through Congress thanks to his oft-praised bipartisanship skills was none other than Senator Joseph Biden, the current president of the United States. Of course, while campaigning for president in 2019 and 2020, he did his best to distance himself from the failed aspects of the controversial bill and how it effectively—unfairly?—targeted blacks. However, notice that black voters once again overwhelmingly threw their votes behind the Democratic candidate—Biden this time.

Go figure. A vast majority of African Americans continue to vote Democrat, and meanwhile the cycle in low-income inner cities repeats itself over and over. Maybe it's time to try something different if you want to change your circumstances. The cops are not the problem that started the Black Lives Matter movement in the first place, even though they get the blame. It's your elected officials who really do not give a crap about you. Memo to Black Lives Matter: that is the reason your systems and your roles never changed.

Let's get back to white privilege. It is a total lie. I'm white; always have been. I grew up in Podunk Nowhere in a family that didn't have a dollar to its name. I came from a broken home, was removed from my family, and had to be raised by my grandparents. My only lifeline for getting out of there was to join the military, and it worked out that I joined during the surge in Iraq. I joined the military knowing that I was going to go to war, which I did twice. I spent a total of thirty-two months in Iraq, then got back to America and started a family. There are untold thousands of military veterans like me, many of whom came from similar backgrounds with modest means, at best. Okay, so where is all this *white privilege* I keep hearing about? Where's my special treatment I'm supposed to get because my skin is white? After twelve years in the military, I was making five grand a month before taxes for a family of five. And I earned every penny of that. That's nothing. Nothing. Nobody gave me anything.

I'm a high school graduate. I do not have a college degree. I got no scholarships. I got nothing. I could have used the GI Bill coming out of the army, but instead I had to work. I didn't have time to go to school. Everything that you see here that I now have—I've worked for every . . . single . . . bit . . . of it. I got no loan from a bank to start my business. No bank would touch me because there's not even an IRS tax code for what we do here; it's still so new. When you form an LLC there isn't a tax code for social media influencing/e-commerce pro America apparel line. No bank will give us any money whatsoever.

White privilege? White supremacy? I mean, what the heck are you talking about? Throwing around terms like that is the sport of losers who are too lazy, apathetic, or entitled to get off their duffs and make something of themselves.

Because I have stood for doing what I do, I don't get big endorsement deals. I have to scrounge and fight for every ounce of revenue, for any sponsorship we can squeeze out of the marketplace, for any kind of sales we can get. I'm under attack constantly because I'm not a PC snowflake. I'm in the news all the time. People come after my family. People threaten my daughter with sodomy, rape, and death. People have threatened me with death, saying that if they ever see me in the street, they're going to put a bullet into my head. Oh, wait, is that what is meant by white privilege—a bullet to the head? Those people who hate me and even threaten me, my business, and my family? Apparently they are Joe Biden's kind of people.

I'll keep my business partner's name out of it, but know this about him: every single person in his family at least has a master's degree. He grew up in a wealthy home, went to West Point, graduated from West Point, served as an officer, got out of the service, and landed an amazing job because he's a very well educated, skilled man. If you were to take our names and faces out of the equation and just went by the descriptions of our backgrounds—and I mentioned this elsewhere in this book—you would assume that he was the white guy and I the black guy in our partnership. Just the opposite.

Black Lives Matter is racist. "All lives matter" is not racist. The problem is, in our society, we think what is good is bad, and it is wrong. If you say the words "All lives matter," you instantly make enemies, and every single one of those enemies is on the left.

If Black Lives Matter actually cared about lives, and if antifa actually cared about people, Black Lives Matter wouldn't burn down communities, wreck black-owned businesses, and kill other black Americans during their riots that they call "protests" or "civil actions." If antifa actually cared about anything, it wouldn't be able to just take over sections of American cities and call them "CHOP" or "CHAZ," sticking supportive weak-minded liberal mayors into their pockets in the process.

They ruin American lives and ruin American businesses, and they don't care. It's all about being heard. At the end of the day, it boils down to selfishness. Black Lives Matter, Inc., is a selfish, entitled, race-baiting organization. Its sole purpose in life is to divide America under the veil of seeking unity, but it's based in Marxist ideology and anti-Christian theologies. The only way that we can heal as America is to understand that all lives matter. The problem with that, though, is that you no longer get to play the victim card because you are no longer more important than anybody else.

You know what? We don't actually want equality in America right now. I don't mean you and me "we." I mean "we" referring to the likes of Black Lives Matter and antifa and the hard-core liberals who fund and enable those groups while helping to drive the anti-American narrative coast to coast. They want people to pay more attention to them than to anybody else. What these groups really want is in no way to be confused with equality. That's *not* equality. Equality is everybody minding their own business, life sucks, and then you die, and anything better than that, you accomplish on your own. That is equality. That's the truth. That's the way it works. That's the way it happens. Everybody has problems. That's called equality.

I know of so many people who have gone bankrupt multiple times, white dudes, and then they've picked themselves back up, started over, and worked their way back to success. That's not because they're white, and it is not because you're black that you're failing. It is your elected officials whom you continue to elect to office, and then they do nothing for you. Why do you keep doing that? The definition of insanity is doing the same thing over and over and expecting a different result. Conservatives take the opposite approach: once they elect someone to office, it's "Show us what you got. If you suck at it, guess what, somebody else is going to primary you, and you're out of here."

The problem is, we are never going to heal America until Americans are no longer afraid to hurt other people's feelings. Nobody will call anything out, out of fear of being canceled because of cancel culture. That is another virus that is killing America. Cancel culture is being fueled by the media. It's being fueled by the Internet. I recently had a preacher come on as a guest, a black preacher, and he talked about the January

6, 2021, Capitol riots. He talked about how much it had hurt him to see a Confederate flag being carried around the halls of the Capitol but during the news account he was watching there was not a single mention of the Black Lives Matter riots that had been going on for more than six months. Conservatives condemned both; the Left condemned only one of those.

The Left would have you believe that the attack it condemned (on the Capitol building) was worse than the other (six months of violent riots in cities across America, with abhorrent cumulative effect), so therefore the latter either didn't happen or is not even in the same category. That's the sort of warped worldview espoused by the likes of MSNBC's "Morning Joe" Scarborough, who attacked conservative political officials and news commentators who, as he saw it, downplayed the Capitol attack while holding it up for comparison against the BLM-orchestrated riots across America. If it's not one Joe messing with us, it's another. Here's what Scarborough (not Biden) said, as quoted on The Wrap: "I know there are idiots on other cable news channels [an apparent slap at Fox News' Tucker Carlson] that will say, 'Well, this mom-and-pop store was vandalized during the summer riots and that's just as bad as the United States Capitol being vandalized. Actually, no, jackass, it's not."

Yes it is, you pompous jerk. Scarborough added, "I am not going to confuse a taco stand with the United States Capitol."

My question to that is: How many hundreds of taco stand–like businesses, and bigger, like those vandalized or destroyed, does it take to equal a few windows broken at the US Capitol? And let's not forget the body count: five dead at the Capitol; more than double that during the Black Lives Matter months-long rampage of 2020, per the *Guardian*, which reported that as of the end of October 2020 a total of twenty-five Americans had been killed during protests and political unrest in 2020.

I find this completely and utterly distasteful to the actual American way of life. That Capitol would not be there and paid for by Americans' tax dollars if it weren't for all those "taco stands" in the first place, you jackass. The Capitol is the people's house, period. Do we need better protections in place to protect certain people, like elected officials? Sure. Of course, we do.

I condemn the riots. They were a horrible thing. Even if I was for it . . . which I am not. It was the worst strategical move ever if you were going to declare civil war to try to take back America; it's as if those who moved onto and into the Capitol building were saying "We're going to tell you exactly where we are. We're going to tell you exactly where we're going to do it. And we're all going to gather in the same spot." Those people gave conservatives a bad name. The few elected officials didn't even have a chance to fight the battle in the courts that we wanted because we walked right into a trap that no one wanted. Reports later came out that Donald Trump said he had ordered ten thousand National Guard troops in advance of the January 6 event and Speaker Nancy Pelosi had turned the request down, saying that it wouldn't look good. Pelosi denied that Trump had made such a request.

It was also reported by the *Washington Post* that the commanding general of the D.C. National Guard, Major General

William Walker, had requested emergency US Army assistance to deal with what was by then happening inside the Capitol after the breach. However, it had taken three hours and nineteen minutes for Walker to get the proper authorization for National Guard troops to enter and secure the Capitol. During hearings in February before Senate committees investigating the January 6 security breach, Robert G. Salesses, a senior Department of Defense official, testified that only the secretary of defense could authorize the use of army troops in a civil matter.

The problem with Black Lives Matter, All Lives Matter, Unicorn Lives Matter, whatever it is that you believe, is that now the government is stepping in, choosing to back one side on the racial issue more than the other side. The government is now choosing to give benefits to one side more than the other side because, in so many words, "The other side has had privilege for so long that now we have to counteract it and make it right by making the Christian white male the most persecuted person in America."

The government is now stepping in and deciding that it knows what's best. It knows what to do: the white business owner, the white man, the white businesses—they can now take hits, while the government needs to give all its attention to minority businesses and minority this and minority that. I've got no problem with that until you start applying it unequally, unfairly. If you really want to make things equal, every person should have an equal opportunity to get it.

I keep asking myself: Where's my white privilege when I'm a white business owner who wasn't a millionaire when I started my businesses? I had to destroy my personal credit to float bills to be able to pay for my employees to have a job, and now that I actually have a business that is flourishing and I want to get an expansion loan from the Small Business Association, it tells me no because my credit is shot. I can't help that. My credit had to be destroyed for us to get to the point we're at now.

Where's the white privilege in that? It's not there.

One thing I didn't mention when I talked about my business partner earlier in this chapter—and I'm still leaving his name out—is that he's married to a white woman. On that subject, he told me something very interesting: "The most vile people about it are other black people. White people don't care. White people have no problems with it whatsoever. It's the black community that has problems with it." He then told me the most amazing thing, which American citizens would do well to grasp. He said, "People no longer know what racism actually is. They are confusing personal preference with actual racism."

What did he mean by that? With people today, it's not the older generations that are having issues with things related to race, such as mixed marriages. It's the younger generations, age thirty and below. They are the ones who have no idea of what life was like for blacks during the civil rights movement, back in the 1960s with Dr. Martin Luther King, Jr. They don't know what it was like for black people who couldn't sit at the front of the bus, who couldn't eat or wash their clothes in certain areas, who had to go around to the back at a restaurant to get their food because they weren't allowed in there. Or when they were finally allowed to sit inside, they could in an area reserved only for blacks with the rest of the establishment for whites only. None of these younger people have any idea what *actual racism* actually is.

"It is racism only when you have a position of power and authority and you use it in a negative way based around the color of somebody's skin." That was once said to me by a black business owner. He said, "You know, people call me the N-word all they want. Is that racist? I don't know. We, as black people, call each other that all the time. And if it's a derogatory term, we probably shouldn't be saying it to each other."

People have the right to say horrible things if they want to. What they don't have is the right to incite violence. They don't have the right to threaten people. But they have the right to be able to say what they want to. Freedom of speech means that you have the freedom to basically tell somebody to eff off. Of course, it works both ways. The other person has the same right to come back at you with comments that might get under your skin.

Again, it is true racism only when you have power and authority over someone. There once was a time when black people could not get loans from a bank because the bank officers would say, "No, we're not giving it to you because you're black." That's racism. On the other hand, the bank loan officer who now says to you, "You've got horrible credit. We can't do it because you not only have horrible credit, but you also have no collateral, and you've got nothing to your name that checks the right boxes."

"You're not giving me the loan because I'm black?"

"No, that's not what I said. I just told you the reasons we're not giving you the loan."

That's not racism. But see what I mean? The second person naturally assumes that his race is working against him, when it wasn't even mentioned by the loan officer. That's fishing for victimhood.

Black Lives Matter is racist because it is saying that one form of life is superior to another and one form of life needs more attention than another. This is not a valid definition of equality. "All lives matter" is the only statement that proves that we actually care about all people equally. The scariest thing to me is the fact that the government is now getting involved in this and siding with the minority instead of the majority of Americans.

The biggest threat to a free society is a government that always believes it's right. And right now, our government believes that some lives matter more than others.

Seven

FACT-CHECKS EQUAL
REAL POWER

*Fact-checkers and fact-checking are part of a ploy to
destroy and discard the conservative public narrative.*

This is an old story that has a new twist.

We all know how brutally one-sided and powerful the media have become in America. That's even before we account for a new arm of the media that has thrown another curveball at fair reporting and free speech. I am referring to the relatively new and conniving art of fact-checking. Media entities not only practice and promote their own various forms of fake news and biased reporting but now employ so called fact-checkers to stick it to opposing voices and viewpoints—i.e., conservative voices and viewpoints—through the unregulated practice of fact-checking.

To say that fact-checking and unscrupulous fact-checkers have gotten out of hand is an understatement. It's apparently not enough for left-leaning mainstream media to pump out fake news, now it must also employ so-called fact checkers who aren't seeking truth but destroying it. It's a high-stakes game in the billion-dollar media industry, where anything goes. It's like what the Ugandan president and murderous despot Idi Amin once said: it is not enough for him to succeed; everyone else must fail.

The relentless mission of this new and diabolical breed of fact-checkers is to tear down and weaken conservative voices by dredging up baseless accusations questioning the veracity of conservative reporters and commentators, such as me. I have to deal with this all the time. I could probably quote directly from the Bible, and there would be at least one fact-checker who would dispute what I said.

This brings me back to Big Tech, the enemy of the people. I'm talking about the Facebooks and Twitters of the world, just for starters. They have plenty of company. They are determined to squelch conservative voices, and their threshold for canceling conservative speech and viewpoints is getting lower all the time. They are getting away with media-oriented murder: maybe it's not "kill the messenger," but it is "kill the message." You don't like what somebody says, writes, or posts? Fact-check them into a corner with a truth twist, make it public with phony facts and fluid so-called standards of your own, and perhaps destroy their credibility. All is fair in love, war, and defining what's truth and what isn't. Pretty sick stuff.

It's time to defund the media and not the police, which is a lose-lose in the eyes of activist groups such as Black Lives Matter and antifa. The media obviously play a hand in this.

They and their fact-checkers are bought and paid for by leftist billionaires and elitists who want to shape the narrative with a wholly progressive bent. If their own liberal-oriented message fails to resonate—and it often does—they believe they can still elevate their credibility (using that term lightly) in the eyes of the public by bashing other media that refuse to play their game of belittling traditional America while pushing a socialist agenda.

A lot of people don't realize the power Big Tech has. And when I say Big Tech, I am specifically referring to *all* the social media apps, not just Facebook and Twitter but also Instagram, Pinterest, and YouTube. We can also include in there the likes of Google and Amazon. After a while, they all just run together; they are like a single humongous entity; it's hard to tell one from another. Not only is each a monopoly in its own right, they could just as well band forces and form their own all-powerful conglomerate. Hey, we are practically there now. In the old days, the saying was "You can't fight city hall." Nowadays, the expression could just as easily be "You can't fight Big Tech." They rule the roost, and most people don't know what's happening behind the scenes.

The last time I checked, former Facebook chief security officer Alex Stamos wasn't a fact-checker, he was worse—someone from the Big Tech media family with enough sway to go on CNN and essentially call for the censorship of conservative speech, with an audience of millions of CNN viewers. In making such a pronouncement in January 2021, predictably unchallenged by his bobblehead CNN hosts, Stamos essentially compared the conservative voice to that of the international terrorist group ISIS, a subject he knows well. Stamos helped Facebook and other social media companies working in tandem with the federal government to boot ISIS from Facebook. Next on the to-be-banned list: conservatives.

As reported by the website Townhall, Stamos told CNN, "I think we need to do a couple of things. One, there needs to be intentional work by the social media companies, collaborating together to work on violent extremism the same way they worked on ISIS. . . . And second, we have to turn down the capability of these conservative influencers to reach these huge audiences. There are people on YouTube, for example, that have a larger audience than daytime CNN, and they are extremely radical in pushing extremely radical views."

There you go: Stamos equating conservative viewpoints to violent extremism. CNN seemed content to lap it up, giving Stamos free rein to spout such nonsense, which in itself *was* worthy of censorship. This is what we're dealing with in America—a one-way street when it comes to being free to say what you believe in. This is our reality as long as the likes of Mark Zuckerberg (Facebook cofounder and CEO) and Jack Dorsey (Twitter CEO) agree with your politically correct slanted point of view. So much for any congressional oversight of Zuckerberg and his ilk; they are worth billions. That explains why the likes of a Democratic-controlled Congress kowtows to Big Tech, like servants to their masters. It bears repeating: "You can't fight Big Tech."

Speaking about CNN, if we really want to get the most out of fact-checkers, a great way to start would be aiming the spotlight at CNN to put its news reporting and punditry under some deserved scrutiny. Consider what Project Veritas (PV) turned up in early 2021 when it taped Charlie Chester, a technical director at the network, spilling the beans on how the network had gone out of its way to do what it could in 2020 to oust Trump from office, even admitting that he wished it had done *more*. Posing as a nurse, the PV investigative reporter went out on several dates with Chester, surreptitiously taping their conversations. The CNN staffer spoke of the network's having targeted Trump's demise by using "propaganda" and hyped covid-19 death numbers to stir up heightened fear among viewers, much of it specifically demanded by CNN president Jeffrey Zucker. Chester told his "date," as the *New York Post* paraphrased it, that Zucker would "call the control room to order producers to play up the Covid death count on-screen."

This is good stuff, an open window showing what goes on behind the scenes—and makes it onto TV and computer screens worldwide—at one of the world's most trusted (said with a straight face) cable news networks. Don't take my word for it. Let's listen in some more on Chester, as reported by the *Post*.

"Fear really drives numbers. . . . COVID? Gangbusters with ratings," he reportedly told the unidentified PV staffer. "Which is why we constantly have the death toll on the side," referencing the covid-19 death tracker shown prominently on-screen, much like the older networks did when reporting on the Vietnam War, giving daily updates on the numbers of soldiers wounded and killed on both sides—the higher the enemy's numbers—good news!!—the closer the United States was to winning what was falsely believed at the time to be a war of attrition. It would make our point better if [the COVID death toll] was higher."

On the subject of propaganda: "Look what we did, we [CNN] got Trump out. I am 100 percent going to say it, and I 100 percent believe that if it wasn't for CNN, I don't know that Trump would have got voted out," Chester said, admitting to the "nurse" that he had gone to work for CNN because he "wanted to be a part of that."

Fake news? Even the insiders responsible for much of it admit it.

The inherent and mandated bias of many if not all liberal media is old hat. I am reminded of when the Air America radio network was launched in March 2004 as a left-wing alternative to conservative talk radio, which at the time dominated listenership ratings with such power hitters as Rush Limbaugh and Sean Hannity. The hope among its backers and staffers was that Air America, with its heavily liberal bias, would effectively counter the conservative narrative and achieve similar ratings success, political influence, and financial windfalls as conservative talk radio. But it was never to be. Not even close.

As *Vanity Fair* magazine reported in 2009, five years after Air America's launch:

Despite abundant publicity and an impressive roster of on-air talent, Air America's ratings never came anywhere near those of right-wing titans such as Limbaugh and Sean Hannity, or even those of heartland progressive Ed Schultz.

To make matters worse, the network was beset by a raft of off-air problems almost from its inception: a charity-loan scandal, contract disputes with affiliates and employees, continual changes in ownership and management, and a 2006 bankruptcy.

The writing was on the wall. A year after *Vanity Fair*'s prescient obituary of Air America appeared on the magazine's pages, Air America was toast, although some of its on-air personalities found jobs and smidgens of success here and there in other ventures. Years later, though, we have the likes of Stamos, Facebook, and Twitter, whose like-minded motto could very well be "If you can't beat 'em, screw 'em over—and get them censored and fact-checked into oblivion." This is an ongoing process—and problem.

This all got started when Facebook as well as Twitter, Instagram, et al. realized that they had a problem—an opposing voice not shy about fighting back. Not only had they given a platform to the people they are in bed with—the far Left, the Democrats, and so on—they also had unwittingly given a platform to the enemy, including ISIS and conservatives. If you aren't liberal, then you must be ISIS or Russian—or even worse, American conservatives, otherwise known as "violent extremists."

In 2016, many Democrats and other governmental folks in Washington blamed Facebook for Donald Trump's election, which wasn't supposed to happen. There were (and are) so many people like myself reaching and influencing millions upon millions of people through our broadcasts, news, and commentaries—together averaging a billion viewers a year—that the left-leaning media had to be asking "How do we go after that? How do you go after conservatives and shut them up?"

Fact-checking and fact-checkers were barely on the radar a year ago; nobody knew what it was or who they were. Oh, there were media fact-checkers at traditional forms of media, such as newspapers and cable TV news, but their scrutiny was usually turned inward. Some of them were called "ombudsmen," tasked by newspapers to give readers a sounding board to handle their complaints and questions about topics such as how stories had been reported and written, with many newspapers running corrections and clarifications daily as needed. Occasionally, the ombudsmen wrote pieces explaining how a story was covered or what editorial policies a newspaper had in place, giving readers an insider's peek from time to time. All of that was self-directed, such that they turned the spotlight on themselves while rarely challenging the factual reporting and editorial presentations of competitors. There is no honor among thieves, and he who is without sin casts the first stone—stuff like that.

In terms of what we are talking about here—fact-checkers as Big Tech weapons to beat opposing voices out of existence— nobody knew what fact-checkers were. Now they do; they pop up on the Internet whenever there is a conservative voice deemed worthy of such harassment. So what do you do to go after people with a voice reaching a large audience—in this case, a conservative voice? You sic fact-checkers on them. But you can't do it yourself, because then people will accuse you of being biased. Instead, you hire or subcontract third-party fact-checkers to do the dirty work for you while giving you plausible deniability of being directly involved, putting "the fix" in.

If you google it, Breitbart is not a fact-checker. Fox News is not a fact-checker. The Daily Wire is not a fact-checker. None of these conservative outlets is a fact-checker. On the other hand, there are the Associated Press and *USA Today*, and there is also a website called Lead Stories. Fact-checkers one and all. I get into it with the Lead Stories fact-checkers at least three or four times a month.

Lead Stories was cofounded by a guy named Alan Duke. He serves as its editor in chief, according to the website, having previously worked twenty-six years for CNN as a reporter focused mostly on entertainment, current affairs, and politics. Alan Duke is a former CNN pundit. So obviously, all those years spent at CNN made him a super-nonbiased professional, a leader in his fact-checker world, right? Not exactly. What's interesting is that whenever you (or I) rebut a fact-check by Lead Stories, Alan Duke is the person who responds to you directly. I'm always honored when it happens to me. I get it right from the top, although you have to think that crap rolls downhill, so guess what ends up at my doorstep whenever Lead Stories comes after me!

Here's the thing about fact-checking entities: they are terrorist organizations. What I mean is that their sole purpose in life is to destroy a voice or voices from the other side, whether it means "blowing up" a particular political figure (a conservative one, of course) or taking down a media organization that has the gall to report something negative about one of their golden icons, such as Joe Biden or Nancy Pelosi. They are perfect, right? Be serious. How do you know when Biden is lying, getting a fact wrong, taking something out of context, making a fool out of himself while misspeaking about someone, or unwittingly poking fun at a minority? When his lips are moving. Even reading from a teleprompter, he gets stuff wrong. But where are the fact-checkers when Biden is around? Probably sleeping on the job.

Fact-checkers don't fact-check Joe Biden. In fact, I think that during the entirety of the presidential debates, President Trump was fact-checked something like 635 times on social media; Joe Biden was fact-checked zero times. Do you mean to tell me that in the entirety of everything Biden said over the course of those debates, there wasn't one thing he said that was either (A) wrong, (B) not his fault, (C) only partly his fault, (D) taken out of context, or (E) outright said to mislead people or change the subject (such as when Hunter Biden's name came up)? The guy is either a liar or just a serial bungler of the facts. Unbelievable but believable.

What a lot of people don't realize is that these organizations target and terrorize conservative figures by scouring through and scrutinizing pages to find things they have said or written to misconstrue. Then they try to ding their accounts and take them out. Like what happened with Parler in early 2021 and the egregiousness that was involved while everyone else just sat there and watched it happen. I even posted something about it: "In three days, they managed to get Parler knocked off the web servers, these web servers still can't figure out how to get child porn off the Internet and keep it off, even though everybody and their uncle has known for years of the presence of Internet child porn and its unsavory presence and effects on people addicted to such things. It's all plain repulsive, and hypocritical."

To this day, there's still something called Pornhub, which has come under fire over the years. The likes of Capital One and Visa won't allow you to make transactions on Pornhub because it does not have standards in place to prevent the distribution of child porn. In fact, this is going to make a lot of people sick, but it's true. I'm not saying people can't watch porn—I'm certainly not suggesting they do watch it—but do whatever you want to do. It's a free country. What a lot of people don't realize is that the nineteen-year-old in the porn you just watched was probably actually fifteen or sixteen years old, if that, and you just didn't know it, right? That's where Pornhub gets into trouble.

In February 2021, a proposed class action lawsuit filed in federal court in Orange County, California, against Mind-Geek, the parent company of the adult website Pornhub, alleged, according to court papers and as reported by NBC, that Pornhub "has violated federal sex trafficking and child pornography laws by . . . profiting from thousands of pornographic videos featuring persons under the age of 18." Further, the complaint made references to Reddit posts, allegedly made by Pornhub's city community manager that verifying the ages of those participating in the videos would be a "disaster" by cutting online traffic in half for the company.

After I wrote the post about how they took down Parler in three days but can't keep child porn off the Internet, fact-checkers took notice and went to work on me, trying to get me straightened out. What fact-checkers do, at least with me and others, is that they write a BS article about whatever topic they have gigged me on and then use that BS article as the basis of and "credible" source by which they determine the truthfulness of what I wrote, even if what they say about me *isn't* what I said or wrote. I got fact-checked for saying that, and the fact-check was by, you guessed it, Lead Stories. Its fact-check said that social media and Big Tech cannot control the distribution of child porn on the Internet. Well, that might be true, but that wasn't what I said. I said that the web servers that house the URLs and the domain names of the websites that do have an influx of an uncontrollable amount of child porn through them still exist, yet they took Parler out in three days. They were able to do that in three days because Parler was too dangerous. They were highly motivated, because Parler is a haven for millions of conservative voices that have become fed up with the politically biased shenanigans of the likes of Facebook and Twitter.

This is how it usually happens. Fact-checkers such as Lead Stories take what we say, which is actually true, and then they fact-check us against a story or article that they just wrote on the spot—the ink isn't even dry yet, so to speak. It's not an article that has existed for years, and it is not histori-cal data they pull from. No, they literally write the article, and then they use it to fact-check you against the article.

Just like the Bible views all sin as sin, Facebook, Instagram, Twitter, and their cousins view all fact-checks as equally credible. So if I get a fact-check saying that something minor I said or wrote was missing context or *could* be missing context and therefore could mislead people—and that sort of thing is wide open to interpretation—I get a ding against my account, just as I would if I were found guilty of actually spreading false information, which, I think you'll agree, is a more serious offense. Here's an interesting aside to all this: I once made a video about how if you typed "antifa.com" into the Google search page, it would take you to the Joseph R. Biden for President website. To this day, March 20, 2021, as I write this, it's still true. Get on your computer right now, type in antifa.com on your search engine, and watch where it takes you. The first thing you should see is Joe Biden in front of a huge US flag. Touching, huh?

Before Biden was president, typing in "antifa.com" led you to Biden/Harris for President. So I made a video pointing this out. On the video, I say, "Look, I'm not saying that Joe Biden is funded by antifa; I'm not saying he's bought by antifa. I'm simply saying that if you type in 'antifa.com,' it takes you to Biden/Harris for President." Well, I got fact-checked for supposedly spreading false information via that video. The article that they used to fact-check me was about Joe Biden not taking money from nor involved with anything related to antifa.com or antifa. So here's my question: How can you say that a video stating that if you type in "antifa.com," it takes you to the website of Joe Biden for president, whitehouse.gov, is spreading false information when that is literally where antifa.com goes? I never said or even implied that Joe Biden is involved in antifa. I only said that if you type in "antifa.com," it goes to whitehouse.gov.

I'm still waiting for the day that Joe Biden gives a news conference and he's asked by one of the reporters, "Mr. President, why does typing in 'antifa.com' in a search engine take you straight to the whitehouse.gov website, and why haven't you done something to fix it?"

That's when his staff will say there are these things called "redirects" and people can easily buy a URL and make it redirect to whitehouse.gov or whatever other website you want to tag. "You mean to tell me that the White House doesn't have the capability to stop a redirect?" Perhaps doing so could be construed as a violation of the First Amendment regarding the government's censorship of free speech, but you can't convince me that a presidential administration lacks the know-how and means to make something like that go away, with its cadre of lawyers standing by to make it stand. Sounds like small potatoes to me. Absolutely, or at least most likely, they do have a capability to stop a redirect, especially if their highly paid attorneys can somehow find a statute or legal precedent that could render a redirect an illegal act in itself. Certainly, these guys and gals weren't asleep the day they taught that in law school. But now let's bring it back to the point: they couldn't take us (conservatives) out just on their own, so they have to take us out by bringing in a neutral third party to decide what is true and what is false.

Let me tell you about another fact-check that has been used on me. I made another video about how the Centers for Disease Control and Prevention (CDC) came out and said that asymptomatic spread of the coronavirus was almost nonexistent—its words, not mine. I just repeated it in the video.

At the time when covid-19 was just getting started, the biggest fear about covid-19 was that people who had it but were showing no signs or symptoms could unwittingly make others sick.

What happened was that the CDC had come out and, good news, it's looking as though the *asymptomatic* spread of the virus is not true and not real. Okay, so I make a video about that, and it goes viral; it's seen by millions of people. Three weeks later, I get a fact-check saying that this is false information. Because four days after I made that video, the CDC clarified its statement and said that what they actually meant to say was that *presymptomatic* people do spread the virus. So now we know that there's a difference between asymptomatic and presymptomatic people, and presymptomatic people *do* spread the virus. So I got dinged because the video I made became outdated four days after I posted it because of the release of new CDC information contradicting what my video reported. Welcome to the world of fact-checking.

So now I have to ask this: Do fact-checkers ever go back and fact-check and ding the accounts of CNN, MSNBC, ABC, NBC, and all these other news outlets that falsely reported that Jussie Smollett was the victim of a hate crime? Do they go back and fact-check all of them because facts do change as things come around? Of course not; they are CNN, MSNBC, etc., after all. You can't fight—or fact-check—city hall.

Now, you might ask, "What's the big deal about a fact-check?" Here's what the average American doesn't understand. Okay, you might get a twenty-four-hour ban or a weeklong ban or even a thirty-day ban on Facebook, but then you can come back right after serving your time. What they don't understand is what it does to people like me, that if you get one ding, you go into the yellow zone. You get two dings, and you go into the red zone. Then if you get another ding after that—well, actually they don't tell you how many dings you're allowed after you go into the red zone, but you're gone. Deleted. Your page is done, over with.

Also, once you go into the red zone, it demonetizes you to the point that you're not allowed to make money. That's important to someone like me because a lot of the stuff that we do is funded by the money we make off the videos we have on Facebook. But this is where they get you and shows you where Facebook stands on things and how it is so smart and determined about what it does. At this point, many people might say, "What's the big deal about demonetization? You can make money other ways as long as you still have your audience and as long as you're still allowed to talk to your audience, right?"

Not so.

If you are demonetized, the Facebook algorithms are designed to allow videos that are monetized to go further, because videos that have money behind them go further, and it makes more money. It makes money off the people that pay for the sponsored ads to go on your video in the first place, so therefore, it lets it go further. Once you're demonetized, however, it takes away your distribution all the way down to 25 percent of your audience. If you become demonetized, it takes away your money, and it takes take away your audience. And it all is at the power of their fact-checkers.

So who fact-checks the fact-checkers? Who has the authority? No one, but you already guessed that. Right now, if I were to be arrested and taken to jail, I would have the right to hire a lawyer. I would have the right to go to trial. I would be innocent until proven guilty, and I'd have the right to defend myself. What they—"they" meaning the likes of Google, Amazon, and Apple, which have the power to shut down an app such as Parler—proved with Parler—and what they're proving with their attacks on conservatives—is that we do not have rights; we do not have the right to do what we want to do and say something the way we want to. And a lot of them like to use the argument "Well, it's a private company" argument.

Is there really any such thing as a private company anymore? Facebook is a publicly traded company. I know that. I can buy stock in Facebook right now if I want to. Doesn't it have to use the Internet? I'm pretty sure Facebook doesn't own the Internet. Doesn't it have to use the cell towers of AT&T, Verizon, T-Mobile, Sprint, and all the other companies as well? I'm pretty sure social media apps don't work very well without the Internet and/or cell towers. So isn't Parler really a private company that should be able to say whatever it is it wants to say and do what it wants to do all the time? I also know this: Who is Facebook to take my money as a business owner of Nine Twelve United? I pay Facebook money; we are in this for that relationship through monetary spending, for advertising.

There's a business called American AF that sells patriotic clothing and gear, and it garnered $35 million a year by selling pro-Trump apparel. All right—it advertised on Facebook, it sold off of Facebook, and so on. So Facebook took money to run sponsored ads. Well, then, when all the stuff with Trump started happening, it took away the company's Facebook page for selling pro-Trump apparel. A $35 million business, and it just jettisoned it like that—*bam!* Gone. Where is the justice in that?

Parler was a great landing place for people who had given up on Facebook and wanted to return to the land of free speech, where conservative viewpoints are welcome and respected. The argument had always been that if you didn't like the policies on Facebook, Twitter, Instagram, or YouTube, you were always free to go somewhere else. But for the longest time, there wasn't anywhere else to go, the Big Tech sentiment being "Well, you're free to create your own platform." So that was what happened; someone created Parler. Big Tech had never anticipated that a new platform could come up and actually start to make a dent. Parler became the number one downloaded app in the Apple App Store before it was taken down. Big Tech's rebuttal went from "You can use other apps" to "You can create your own apps" to "You can create your own Internet." That's what it was essentially saying. And Parler was succeeding, much to the dismay of Facebook and the others. The question is, though, if Parler is a private business and therefore should be allowed to do whatever it wants to do, why was it not allowed to operate? Why was it killed in a matter of days?

★ ★ ★

The controversy about Big Tech, social media, freedom of speech, and, most recently, fact-checking and fact-checkers boils down to Section 230 of the federal Communications Decency Act, which was passed with bipartisan support in 1996. This was at a time when what you could call social media—in those days associated with young, high-tech companies such as Prodigy—was in its infancy. But the Internet was showing a remarkable potential that proponents saw as 100 percent upside and safe enough to be worthy of preferential treatment. Section 230 was aimed at protecting what we now know as "Big Tech" media companies—that since have come to include the likes of Facebook, Twitter, and Instagram—from the same sort of liability restrictions borne by publishers, such as newspapers, regarding publication of content relative to issues such as libel. In essence, Section 230 was a means of allowing social media the opportunity to flourish, promoting an unprecedented forum of worldwide communications, such as bringing together high school or college classmates who hadn't spoken to one another in decades.

In a nutshell, Section 230 not only protected Big Tech companies from legal liability for content posted on their sites, it also gave them the exclusive right to remove posted content it deemed in violation of their own standards—providing they were acting in "good faith." In a retrospective October 2020 *New York Post* article summarizing the implications of Section 230 over the past twenty-plus years, reporter Gabrielle Fonrouge wrote:

> More than two decades later, critics of the law say it has been interpreted in the courts well beyond its

original intent and has handed private tech companies the keys to the modern day version of the public square. Politicians on both sides of the aisle agree
Big Tech has immense power that needs to be reigned
[*sic*] in and regulated while some want to repeal Section 230 altogether. . . .

But in the 24 years since it was passed, the law—
and the way the courts have interpreted it—has
bloated it well beyond its original intent and has also
allowed for a much darker corner of the Internet to
thrive, said Carrie Goldberg, a Brooklyn-based lawyer and an outspoken critic of Section 230.

The *Post* was referring to Goldberg's advocacy for people whose lives have been ruined by the presence of revenge
porn, child sexual exploitation, and stalking that has found a
haven on the Internet and social media, usually hidden in the
"darker corner" cited by the *Post*. "These companies have no
obligation to have safe products that are free from child sexual abuse material and stalking," Goldberg said, quoted by
the *Post*. "It means that . . . when there's a serial rapist that's
using Match.com, even if Match.com knows that a registered
sex offender is using their platform, they would argue that
they have no liability to anybody that gets raped by this person because of Section 230."

Section 230 is what protects the social media giants,
allowing them to be virtually invulnerable to lawsuits. That's
why all of the people who have tried to take them to court and

tried to go all the way to the Supreme Court with Facebook have been shut down—because of Section 230.

When Section 230 went into effect in 1996, it was still in the days of dial-up Internet, most often associated with America Online, and before what we know as social media, at least in today's model, came into existence. As stated above, the purpose of Section 230 was basically to say that Internet sites are not liable for what other people might say on the Internet. Like you can't help it if somebody says something that incites violence on the Internet—you can't be held liable for that. Yet Parler got held liable for that. What 230 has been transformed into is a loophole that has allowed social media to become protected from lawsuits, and that makes them invincible. Believe it or not, this is one area on which former president Donald Trump and current president Joe Biden have agreed: the social media giants should lose their Section 230 protections.

Big Tech is bigger than the government. The proof was in the censoring and the banning of President Trump at the time when he was still President Trump. Facebook, Instagram, Twitter, YouTube, Shopify, PayPal, and other platforms effectively said that they are more powerful than the most powerful man in the world. No, you can't talk to the people anymore; can't do it. Can't speak to the people, can't talk to the people, you are too dangerous, and we can't allow you to do it.

Yet the ayatollah is still allowed to tweet. Elements of the Chinese Communist Party are allowed to post tweets about its concentration camps and sterilization of women and how it's got a pretty good program going—until enough conservatives *finally* got Twitter to delete them. One such tweet, which originated inside the Chinese Embassy in Washington, D.C., in January 2021, boasted that Chinese government policies—apparently referring to state-mandated birth control measures imposed on Muslim minority women had liberated them from having to serve as "baby-making machines." A Chinese official quickly denied government involvement in any sort of coerced birth control on women, but who's to say who's telling the truth here? The point is, that tweet was made. Those types of things are perfectly fine, at least much of the time. Yet Big Tech company is going to stand up to the Chinese government and knock it offline, either temporarily or permanently? No dice. Yet they can just say "no" to the most powerful man in the world, the president of the United States. And we've already talked about the Hunter Biden scandal, referring to the current president's son's alleged involvement with Ukraine and China that included reports of his being paid millions of dollars for influence peddling that allegedly also involved his father as well as introductions Hunter Biden brokered with other key figures and how what was being reported by the *New York Post* was suppressed by Big Tech.

Why are the social media giants more powerful than our government? How did this come to be? Why would our government not want to do anything about it? Why can't the government either repeal or amend Section 230 to put some restraints on social media, the Big Tech giants? The scariest part is that either it doesn't want to do it or it is in cahoots with

Big Tech. Social media need Congress; Congress needs social media. *You scratch my back, I'll scratch yours.*

Why do they need each other? Because in 2021, if you don't have a social media presence, you have nothing. What I mean by this is that social media is able to limit the voice of our elected officials. If our elected officials try to talk about things that Big Tech doesn't want them to talk about, it censors them, it silences them, it suppresses their reach. It disables their tweets, it takes away their ability to communicate with the people who elected them in the first place. Also, if you don't have a social media presence and you're not able to advertise on social media and you're not able to get your message heard or your videos seen, then guess what: you're not going to be elected.

Big Tech has our elected officials in its pocket by force and control. If Big Tech is your enemy, you're not going to win ever again. It holds your position and your power in the palm of its hand. That is why the government is never going to do anything about it: because they're in it together, either by choice or by force. Big Tech has become the enemy of the people and the bane of our democracy. If you're not able to talk, if you're not able to express your thoughts, if you're not able to express your feelings in an open forum, then you know it's over and Big Tech has won.

Facebook, Instagram, Microsoft, Apple—these Big Tech companies run the world; they control everything. Microsoft owns the US government. Every single program and system that we used in the military was made by Microsoft. What can we do as Americans when the main way we can communicate in 2021 is through social media? That's the biggest problem I have with the Capitol riots.

Regarding the Capitol riots of January 6, 2021, in DC, people say to me things like "Well, Graham, you were anti the Capitol riots." I was. I was against the Capitol riots, because (A) I didn't believe we were at that point yet, and (B) it was the worst attempt to overthrow anything I've ever seen. It's already been proven that it was preplanned, reports of which can be found in abundance on the Internet. It had nothing to do with anything the president said regardless of whatever politically oriented "conclusions" any investigation of it after my writing this chapter turns up. It would have happened whether Donald Trump had said anything or not. As reported by *Forbes*, Trump "supporters" involved in the storming and breach of the Capitol had been planning to do so for weeks, using social media websites and online forums to discuss violent action. Such advance communication left many observers of the January 6 events wondering why Capitol and Washington, D.C., law enforcement wasn't better prepared. Posts well in advance of January 6 that mentioned possible violence if Trump-supported legal challenges failed to stop Congress's certification of Joe Biden's victory in the November presidential election appeared on many parts of the Internet. The landing places included apps and forums favored by followers of Parler, Telegram, and TheDonald, as well as mainstream platforms such as TikTok and Twitter. Forbes reported numerous instances of other online preplanning, such as a Parler post dated December 23—a full two weeks ahead of the January 6 attack—in which Stop the Steal movement founder Ali Alexander wrote, "We came up with the idea to occupy just outside the CAPITOL on Jan 6th. . . . If D.C. escalates . . . so do we."

Prior to the protestors congregating at the Capitol building and well before some of the protestors breached the building, Trump gave a long speech to his supporters. In it, he went back through dozens of instances from election day that demonstrated voter fraud in key states, at one point in the speech telling the protestors to let their voices be heard but to do so in an orderly and peaceful fashion. Here's an excerpt from the complete transcript as reported by Associated Press and published by *U.S. News & World Report*:

> Now, it is up to Congress to confront this egregious assault on our democracy. And after this, we're going to walk down, and I'll be there with you, we're going to walk down, we're going to walk down.
>
> Anyone you want, but I think right here, we're going to walk down to the Capitol, and we're going to cheer on our brave senators and congressmen and women, and we're probably not going to be cheering so much for some of them.
>
> Because you'll never take back our country with weakness. You have to show strength and you have to be strong. We have come to demand that Congress do the right thing and only count the electors who have been lawfully slated, lawfully slated.

I know that everyone here will soon be marching over to the Capitol building to peacefully and patriotically make your voices heard.

My biggest problem with what happened on January 6 is that we as conservatives walked hook, line, and sinker into antifa, Black Lives Matter, and a corporate plan to make *us* look like the enemy. We walked right into it.

How do you fight back against Big Tech and mainstream media in general, with its fake news machinery and censorship of all voices that run counter to the liberal, progressive fraudsters? My first thought was to band together with other conservatives and do a ninety-day boycott of Facebook or a ninety-day boycott of this, that, or the other, but we can't do that because they will just wait us out and go on doing business as usual.

If you're going to fight back against the media, its censorship of an opposing narrative, and its use of unscrupulous fact-checkers, I think we should start with an Internet 2.0. Go with me here. What is Internet 2.0? Let me answer that by starting with what Internet 1.0 was. It was everybody having access to everything all the time. TV is the same way: everybody has access, everybody can see everything, everybody can do this. Well, what happened was that it gave everybody an opinion and everybody a voice. Unfortunately, that turned into a bad thing because cancel culture arose out of that. What needs to happen now, with Internet 2.0, is people actually starting to put their money where their mouth is. Internet

2.0 would look a lot more like paid subscription services, similar to what you are seeing more and more on the TV side, with streaming services popping up all over the place, each shaping its programming and offerings to a specific blend of audiences. Cable networks are saying, "Well, we're not going to be a part of AT&T or DirecTV anymore. We're just going to have our own streaming service. And people that want to watch us will subscribe and stream these streaming services." I see that happening with Internet 2.0.

At the time I am writing this, in March 2021, word has just come out that Trump is preparing to launch his own social media platform within "two or three months," which would put it into late spring/early summer 2021. Interviewed on Fox News' *#MediaBuzz* on Sunday, March 21, Trump senior adviser Jason Miller said, "And this is something that I think will be the hottest ticket in social media, it's going to completely redefine the game, and everybody is going to be waiting and watching to see what exactly President Trump does."

That's part of what I'm talking about—the emergence of more alternatives to put some pressure on Facebook and Twitter with a healthy competitor that is sure to cut into their market and maybe even provide an entirely new Internet entity that would be an umbrella organization for a variety of subscription-based communities linked together on one vast network. What I see is an Internet 2.0 that will no longer be the World Wide Web—it will be its own self. I think this Internet 2.0 will include community after community that together will offer a robust smorgasbord of online access points that will conceivably give everybody what they want without fear of being canceled or bullied out of existence by the likes of Facebook.

We need to take more charge of all this instead of having it dictated to us by a monopoly that is out of control and running rampant, saturated with power. Then we—you and me—will become the sponsors. You will become the person who's in charge because you will put your money where your mouth is.

At some point, talk has to become action.

Eight

EQUALITY DOESN'T ALWAYS EQUAL BEING EQUAL

"We no longer want equality of opportunity. We now want equality of outcome."

I want to talk about equality and what it actually means, not what the Left has distorted it to mean. Somehow, somewhere along the way, parts of America have given rise to a distorted meaning of equality, something that our socialist-leaning leftists insist means everyone having an equal amount of money, materials, houses, cars, cabin getaways, toys, and other things, even if that outcome requires a mass redistribution of wealth to make sure that no one is left behind and everybody has as much in hand as all of his or her neighbors and beyond, to the rest of America.

You are absolutely correct: this is about as nutty as it gets. Let me explain . . .

First, Webster's dictionary defines *equality* as "the state of being equal, especially in status, rights, and opportunities."

Nowhere—and I mean nowhere in the world and not just in Webster's—does it say that if I have a million dollars in savings and a home worth $400,000 and you have zero savings and a home worth $100,000, we have to balance out what we have. That would mean I have to give you $500,000 in cash, tear down both homes, and build in their place two similar homes each worth $250,000—one for you and one for me—because the Declaration of Independence has declared us "equal" in the eyes of God.

You want a bigger or better house and a savings account with money in it? Go out and earn it. If you want a better, higher-paying job to make those things possible, then get better at what you do. Give your boss a good reason to promote you and pay you more (and if that takes you into a higher tax bracket, so be it; deal with it).

There is a hard truth that no one will ever tell you, certainly not your duly elected Democratic mayor, representative, senator, or president. The truth is, there really is no such thing as being equal, at least not in the manner in which society will have you believe. Are we all equal in the image of God, created in His image to magnify Him? Of course we are! Are all Americans given the same opportunity to undertake the "pursuit of happiness" that is laid out in the Declaration of Independence? You bet we are! However, equality of person or opportunity does not equal equality of outcome! To say that it does is very much a lie! And I'm not sorry about being the messenger who breaks that news to you. And just so we are clear, Webster's defines a *lie* as "an intentionally false statement."

With that out of the way, let's travel to the land of the hard truths and realities of the entire mess surrounding equals and equality that has been created in our society. As we saw in the last seven months of 2020, riots in the streets, the burning of buildings, attacks on the innocent, teardowns of statues of historical figures, and pushing agendas of socialism run rampant in America. That happened because of the basic lie that has befuddled many Americans, who have been brainwashed into believing that equality equates equality of outcome.

This falsehood is continually fed into the American psyche by politicians who operate by the credo that the ends justify the means; anything goes. What comes to mind is an ad that then senator Kamala Harris ran when she was running for president. It was an animated ad showing two people starting to climb a mountain. One was some distance behind the other, with the one in front reaching the top faster than the other person could. Harris's point was that just because we are "equal" doesn't mean we all start from the same place. Her point, although not terrible in principle, was still based on a false pretense—equality of outcome is not found in the Constitution. That makes it unconstitutional.

Some of you might have seen that video and thought *Oh, that is powerful* or *That is so true,* and when you heard her point, you agreed. I can understand if you were one of those nodding their heads in agreement, but let's take a moment to dissect the video. This is so I can straighten something out for you. Let's say it wasn't a video made for a political commercial to make you believe and feel certain things and instead call it a depiction of real life. Two people are at the base of a mountain. They are both professional rock climbers and have trained their entire lives for this event. They have dreamed about it. They even follow a diet based on climbing mountains to help them be the best mountain climbers the world has ever seen. All things being equal, all things are equal here.

So what happens in real life when someone says, "Go, start climbing!" Honestly ask yourself: What happens? If you find yourself stuck looking for an answer: the two do not reach the top at the same time. In fact, one might be so far ahead of the other that the outcome is not even close. This is real life, despite Harris's attempt to make it look like a mistake.

Here's what equality means: that we are all equal under God. No person is more valuable than another person or more loved or favored by God. My problem with all this is that everything the Left tries to do is based on a fundamental lie. Do I believe that all Democrats are horrible people? No. Do I believe that they're all misguided? Yes. The fundamental lie is that a utopian society is possible. It's based on the assumption that people are inherently good, even though the Bible teaches us the exact opposite. People are inherently bad, and it is only through God's grace that we can fight against our inherently bad tendencies.

Think about it from the example of a newborn baby, the most innocent of innocents. That baby doesn't care about anything but itself: feed me, change me, make me feel good. Kids are the same way. It's our job as parents to teach them to nip their selfish tendencies in the bud and proceed toward selflessness. People are inherently not good. In fact, they are inherently bad. That's why confusing equality with equality of outcome is socialistic.

Need another example? Take the same scenario described in the Harris ad and this time substitute runners, except this time let's make the race even more insanely equitable. Say you have three runners, all born in the same place, from the same family, following the same diet, undergoing the same training and conditioning, and allotted the same amount of rest and money. Literally, everything about all three of them is equal in every single way possible, even in ways I don't list here. What happens on race day?

I think you already know the answer. But let me remind you of a scene from one of my favorite movies as a kid. *Cool Runnings* was a movie about the first Jamaican bobsled team, and it starts with a race at a track meet. The main character, a runner who is a shoo-in for the Olympics, takes off running, and everything is going just as planned until someone trips and falls and takes him down with him. It was supposed to have been his race. He was supposed to win and go to the Olympics, but life doesn't always work out that way.

Back to my illustration. All three of our runners take off at the same time, but no matter how equal each of the three is to the other two at the start, one is going to pull ahead! Happens every time. There are very few photo finishes in track. More than likely, one runner is going to break the tape first and clearly win, someone else is going to finish second, and the third runner will finish third and perhaps even fall along the way and not even finish. Remember this: equality can sometimes mean that we all have an equal opportunity to fail. This false kind of equality thinking is a lie that is a gateway into socialism. Looking through a false lens is exactly what the Democrats are doing. The truth of the matter is, there are going to be bosses. Everybody can't be a boss, because then nothing will get done. There has to be a hierarchy. There has to be an order of who's in charge. Not everyone can finish in first place.

Before we go down the road revealing the way Harris's message is part of a dangerous precedent—disparaging competition and innate superiority—let's take a step back so I can talk to you about what hard work actually is, a topic I briefly touch on in the following chapter. Back we go to 2016, when I had just started my daily rants and had absolutely no clue what I was doing. I had no idea how to withhold my taxes, form an LLC, create and maintain profit-and-loss sheets, get sponsors, or make money. All I knew was that I was on to something and I had to figure it out for me and my family.

Most people do not know this, but I left my twelve-year army career for a six-month, $3,500-a-month sponsorship to either "figure things out" or end up broke and without a job after those six months were up. Over the next four years, most of you already know what happened, or you wouldn't be reading this book. We are one of the top conservative voices in the nation. We have one of the top podcasts in the world. I have spoken in person to hundreds of thousands of people across the United States and billions around the world. I am now a serial entrepreneur with multiple businesses, each with revenue in the millions of dollars.

I do not say this to brag! I tell you this because you need to know what it took to get here. You need to hear about my so-called white privilege and the total lie that is. You need to hear about all the other people who were just like me and who didn't make it. You need to hear the whole story. You need to hear everything, all of which is pretty much laid out in this book.

To reiterate, we have perverted equality to mean equality of outcome, which is not only inherently false but also inherently unattainable. It doesn't matter what you do. It doesn't matter how much you try to rig the system. It doesn't matter how many opportunities you give people, whether it's the same amount of money or stimulus checks or whatever it might be. If you give every single person the same opportunities, the same tutors, the same workout routines, the same meal plans, the same rest times, the same video games, the same opportunities across the board, when it comes time to actually perform, one's going to pull ahead.

The analogy also applies to team sports, such as football. There are football teams that work hard for months and months. On paper, one team is superior in every way, shape, form, and fashion, but then on game day, through the outcome of what is called life, an upset happens—and underdog beats its heavily favored opponent. Sometimes it's something you would find almost impossible to imagine, like the 1980 "Miracle on Ice," when the US hockey team beat the far superior Soviet team in the semifinals en route to winning the gold medal. Still, nothing we do is ever going to make us truly equal in the terms of what the outcome is.

Some years ago, the National Football League (NFL) even announced that it would make rules changes with the expressed intent to achieve "parity" in the league—to, in effect, bridge the talent gap between the league's best teams and its worst teams. To some degree it has succeeded. Some franchises that had been bottom dwellers for years became more competitive and even made it to the Super Bowl, and vice versa, with former perennial powerhouse teams occasionally wading through stretches of mediocrity. But anyone who actually believed that parity meant that every team would finish the regular season with an 8–8 record every year—teams play sixteen regular-season games—was sorely mistaken. In any given season, a few teams will finish 12–4 or better and others will end the season 4–12 or worse. It's the way of the world. Ebb and flow.

Equality in America simply says that as an American, you are entitled to the same rights, freedoms, and opportunities as every other American. That's it. But what we're doing now is wanting every American who frankly doesn't deserve it to have the same outcome as Americans who have earned things. Or to be paid the same amount of money. I recently saw something comparing National Basketball Association (NBA) superstar LeBron James with Women's National Basketball Association (WNBA) superstar Sue Bird. Their playing careers were almost an exact match in terms of seasons played (seventeen) and league championships (four), and each had won multiple individual awards, yet LeBron's annual salary was $37 million and Bird's $215,000. That doesn't seem fair at first glance and the wage disparity seems outrageous, but then you have to account for the significant discrepancies between the two leagues, including factors such as audience viewership and TV rights fees, merchandise sales, and league branding and sponsorships. The disparities are astronomical.

I don't particularly think any sports athletes should be making $37 million a year to play a game, but that's a whole different conversation for another time. I say, take all that money, cut it in half, and pay our cops more. The point is, if you're going to say that women in sports should be paid the same amount as men in sports, then isn't it only right that women's sports should pull in the same amount of money that men's sports are pulling in? This has nothing to do with inequality of gender or sexism or misogyny or anything like that. It has to do with the number one thing: money. That's it. It doesn't have to do with racial divide or gender tensions. It has to do with simple mathematics. That is the truth. This is why not everybody make fifteen dollars an hour in his or her job. It's not because we don't want people to live their best lives (assuming that your best life can be had for fifteen bucks an hour).

If you want to talk about really being equal, if you want to talk about equality, what we're really talking about is race and gender. So what do we do about biological men now identifying as women? Do we let them play girls' or women's sports, where they can dominate and ruin women's sports? What does that have to do with promoting equality?

Women athletes want to be paid more money, but be careful what you wish for. Let men who identify as women compete as women, and sure enough, they'll probably start breaking records and then more ad revenue will come in as more sponsors come in. Women athletes will get what they want—more money—except it won't really be women who will be paid more money, it will be the men who identify as women. President Trump said it best: if we continue to let this go, we continue to let this slide.

Coaches want to win games. They don't care what color you are, they probably don't even care what gender you are. If you're better, you're going to get a spot on their team. If transgender men are allowed to compete in women's sports, no coach is going to recruit an actual woman to play on his team, because what's going to happen is that there will be actual women's teams versus teams with an intermix of women and transgender males or transgender females, whatever it is they're called, I don't even know. I can't keep up with it.

You don't really want equality. What they really want is for everybody to have the same thing whether they deserve it or not. The truth of the matter is, there are hierarchies and structures within a society. You might not agree with this, you might not even like it, but it's how societies exist and it's how they've existed for whether you believe the world is thousands of years old or if you believe the world is millions of years old.

When it comes down to it, I know many women who make more money than I do doing the exact same thing. Don't tell me that I have some white male privilege. I look at women on Fox News every day; they do the exact same thing as me, and they're making four, five, ten times as much money as I make.

So don't tell me that the system is rigged. The system isn't rigged. Maybe you just suck and somebody is better than you.

American Idol started this. It was one of the worst things that's ever happened to America. Why? Let me explain. *American Idol* made its biggest ratings in the beginning because viewers wanted to see all the horrible people on stage performing, just like going to a stock car race and waiting for the crashes. People don't tune in to *American Idol* to listen to the good performers. They tune in because they want to see the train wrecks. Those mishaps-in-waiting started going on national television at first; not now. Now it's a publicity stunt, and people want to get their Instagram handles up. But at first, people started going there because we had mommies and daddies who didn't tell their sons or daughters that "Actually, you kind of sound like a cat that's being assaulted by an engine somewhere." Nobody told them that.

Same thing with high school jocks, such as football players. Most of them have delusions of grandeur—or at least college football or NFL stardom—and their parents and pals feed into their egos, telling them all the time how great they are. This is nothing new; it has been going on for decades. At the same time you're hearing guys who are seniors in high school saying they don't want to join the military "because it's my senior year, and I've got football this year and I'm waiting to see if I get offered." Okay, but listen to me, guys: If you haven't been offered already, guess what—you're not going to be playing college football. If you haven't been offered a football scholarship and made a commitment by the end of your junior year, you're probably not going to be playing college football, at least not on a full ride.

False expectations; they permeate our society. Even the music industry has changed. Once upon a time, if you had potential, you would be heard and contacted by talent scouts. Same thing with athletes. With music artists, talent scouts would go around and they'd listen in bars and they'd find people who were diamonds in the rough. And then they would sign them to a major label and turn them into superstars. The Backstreet Boys, NSYNC, Britney Spears—that's what happened with all those people. They found out they could sing a little bit, and then they were made into superstars. It's not that way today. If you don't already have an album, if you don't already have sales, if you don't already have a massive following on Instagram, Twitter, Facebook, or YouTube and are unable to sell out shows, guess what you're not getting? You're not getting a record deal. It has nothing to do with your being black, white, yellow, purple, man, woman, alien, whatever it is you identify as. It has to do with the way the world actually works. The problem is, people don't want to deal with the way the world actually works. They want to deal with equality of outcome. They want the same things as the people who have what they want. That's it. They don't want to work for it. They don't want to have to earn it. They just want.

There is want all over America—tens of millions of people wanting and expecting things to be given to them, for job promotions and pay raises to be given to them. If somebody has or is getting something that somebody else wants, other people believe that just because they want it, they deserve to have it. It's pitiful.

Something else that falls into that category is the move within our country to raise the federal minimum wage for nonexempt employees from $7.25 an hour to $15, more than double. Well, what can go wrong there? Rising waters raise all ships, right? Not exactly, but this proposal has legs and at this writing was still being bounced around among Washington's politicos. The $15-an-hour thing is something that's been going on for a long time, but I don't see it going anywhere. Fifteen bucks an hour is called "a living wage" because that's what Vermont senator and two-time presidential candidate Bernie Sanders calls it. It is yet another attempt at redistributing wealth or in this case redistributing payrolls among companies, but it is a bad move because it will lead to the elimination of jobs within companies and add to our unemployment rolls.

It won't work. The average everyday American has absolutely no idea what it is like to own, operate, and continue a business in any way, shape, form, or fashion. Doubling the minimum wage, even if the increase is phased in over a period of several years, will be especially devastating to small-business owners who simply don't have the buffer in their already stretched-thin budgets to absorb the increase in payroll that will hit them. They will have to lay off employees. Even further, average Americans really should just shut their mouths about things they do not understand at all, such as being responsible for running a small business. For one thing, it truly is a 24/7 proposition. I know that sounds really harsh and is such a mean thing for me to say, but it is true.

Four years ago, I wasn't a business owner. I was just a guy in a beat-up F-150 pickup truck screaming his opinions into a phone. That was my life as a business owner just starting out, trying to survive, trying to get into the black and stay there. Out of that has come a multibusiness, multi-employed-people, multi-having-to-pay-taxes-in-the-hundreds-of-thousands-of-dollars-every-single-year-type business. Just as the way the world should actually work, my opinions have changed, evolving into the truth of what the realities are. Yes, I believe that there are a lot of people who are underpaid for what they do. On the other hand, do I believe that every single person should make $100,000 a year? Absolutely not. Not only is it not possible, it also is not economically stable, it also is simply not true.

Not every single person deserves a $15 minimum wage job. Let's talk about the reality of what a $15-an-hour living wage would actually do to businesses. The unfortunate part about this is that the only people who know this and who understand this are people who own businesses. A $15-an-hour living wage isn't an improvement. In fact, it's the exact opposite.

This goes along with the lie of the utopian society that we've talked about in this entire book. The Democrats operate under the utopian concept that if they just do this, life is going to be fantastic. They don't look at budgets, they don't look at realities, and they don't look at truths. A $15-an-hour minimum wage doesn't lead to a better-paying job. It leads to no job.

I own an apparel company. One of the biggest questions that we hear every single day is "Oh, are your products made in America?" Every single person who asks that question is the same person who will not pay a more expensive price for a T-shirt that is made in America. The vast majority of Americans don't make enough money to be able to afford products that are made in America. People are cheap; they want whatever is the cheapest option available of whatever it is they want to buy, and this lie and this illusion go right into the proposed $15 an hour. Fifteen dollars an hour sounds good on paper because $7.25 is the federal minimum wage, which, I admit, is too low. When I came out against it, saying "This is going to tank the economy, and this is going to destroy jobs, not build more jobs," people responded with "Graham, it's the $15 *federal* minimum wage, that applies only to federal employees." Yes, that is a real statement I heard from someone. What the federal minimum wage does is stipulate that employers in none of the fifty states can pay an employee less than the federally mandated amount.

If you sense anger or irritation in my words, it's simply because I deal with these people every single day. These are the people who vote Democrat and who vote for this policy even though it will actually tank the economy. This shows that they have no idea what they are talking about. They don't even know what the federal minimum wage actually is.

Every state is different. Some states have already set the minimum wage at $15 an hour or more. By raising the minimum wage to $15 an hour nationwide, though, you're going to kill jobs. In places like South Carolina and Mississippi and other lower-income-level economies, many employers will not be able to afford it. Period. This isn't guesswork or trying to shoot a hole in a left-supported move, it's basic math. Find a small-business owner who employs five or more people and has an annual net profit margin of less than 5 percent. Then pull out your calculator and do the math, based on his or her profit-and-loss statement. It's not pretty. That's a reality, and math, that most Democrats are too stupid or stubborn to understand.

Now let's talk about McDonald's. Its workers are famous for demanding $15 an hour. McDonald's is one of my favorite companies because about two years ago, when rumors of that started happening, the company slapped employees in the mouth by installing automated machines that allow customers to type in their order themselves. So now there are mostly managers working there, making something like $12 an hour. All they have to do is look at the little screens and put together whatever customer's orders have been sent to them. They put the food together and hand you your bag. Simple as that.

So, you ask, what are some other real-world repercussions for this? As I said, I own an apparel company. Right now, we sell, on average, a T-shirt at $29.99. That's the not-made-in-America version. If you want the made-in-America version, that T-shirt jumps up to about $38.99. This is at the minimum wage now set at $7.25 an hour. If you increase the minimum wage to $15 an hour, the not-made-in America T-shirt will jump up to about $38.99 and the made-in-America one will jump up to probably around $50. Trust me when I say you don't even want to know what the hoodies would cost.

The simple truth is that customers are not going to pay that price and therefore won't buy the T-shirts, and what will that do to the owner of the apparel company? Now the company is not making sales, it's not making money. So who are the first people that are going to be laid off? The people that are making $15 an hour.

The simple truth of the matter is that making $15 an hour the new federal minimum wage doesn't do anything but make $15 the new $7.25. That's all it does. You're now going to be paying $6 for a gallon of milk. Your gas prices are already starting to rise. Even before Joe Biden killed the Keystone pipeline immediately upon taking office, gas prices already started to rise. Welcome back, $5, $6 a gallon in California. Places like California that already have the higher-end minimum wage—what will their new minimum wage be after the minimum $15-per-hour wage for all fifty states is put into place? Will California's minimum wage go higher? Maybe to $30 an hour? Forty? Fifty? Remember, the mandate is for a *minimum* wage—it doesn't place any limit on how high a state wants to take it to help compensate for the accompanying spike in the cost of living. You want to talk about the cost of the dollar just disintegrating? Just because you call it a living wage, that doesn't mean it's actually going to be a living wage because the government is mostly by young people under the age of twenty-eight, and they have no idea what they're doing.

Next, let's talk about the stock market and what's been going on there. Keep in mind, when we are talking about all this, that even though we have shifted to financials as the focus of this chapter, all these issues play directly into the concept of equality not meaning equal being equal. We're still sitting squarely in the middle of things like individual

entitlement and a severely flawed manner in which Democrats define things such as equality and opportunity versus
outcome.

Here's the deal with the stock market and how it plays
into all this: the deck is stacked against everyday Americans
across the board, no matter what it is, no matter who you are,
no matter what you do, no matter what you think, no matter what you feel. Whenever AOC (Representative Alexandria
Ocasio-Cortez, D-NY) and Senator Ted Cruz (R-TX) agree
with each other on something that's going on, you know that
something big has taken place, right?

Wall Street has been an enemy of everyday American people pretty much since its beginning. There is nothing about
Wall Street that is geared toward the everyday person—me,
you, Jim down the road, or Susan who works at the hair salon.
However, one day in early 2021, an amazing thing happened
on Reddit and some other online resources including chat
rooms and message boards. Everyday folks sort of manipu-
lated Wall Street. They got into the system and started buying
up penny stocks in companies such as GameStop and AMC
that had been pretty much killed by covid-19. The idea was to
invest in and buy up all the nearly worthless stocks of those
companies, and jack the prices up, and then short sell them.

What ended up happening was that there were all these
everyday Americans buying shares and cashing out in short-
sale stock options, making millions of dollars by manipu-
lating the stock market. Which is exactly what Wall Street
insiders have been doing pretty much the entire time over
the years. Except this time, it was average Janes and Joes who

figured out a way to circumvent the system to make money for themselves, everyday Americans. Call it an equal opportunity bonanza for those average Americans, a redistribution of some wealth in their favor. A victory for the small guy or gal, right?

Not exactly. What did Wall Street do? It shut everything down—every single stock-trading option, such as the Robinhood investing app, that you can think of. In fact, Robinhood has already been sued over this because it was such an egregious attack against the American people—the commoners. It was a way of telling average-Joe investors that they were destroying the hedge fund base. There are all these hedge fund millionaires and billionaires who are normally in the stock market, with their millions invested all over the place to make money, and now "You are destroying them, so therefore, we cannot allow you to do it."

"Shut the trading in GameStop down!" And Robinhood did.

It's shut off the ability for people to put their name into the game by buying stock in companies that are low-priced and watching the stock price soar, then selling the stock to make a profit. That is supposed to be the entire purpose of the stock market, without prejudice. You risk your money investing in companies: you buy when the stocks are low and sell when they are high. That's just how the system works, right? Investors make your money that way. But only the "right" people, apparently.

The only people who are allowed to do this, apparently, are the rich and the elite. Because the second the average

American starts doing it, the second the average American starts making headway and figuring out the system, well now the market is too volatile. And now they can't allow this to happen. Why? It's not because they care about Americans risking their own money being grown adults taking chances for themselves; it's because they are disrupting the system. Let's see Kamala Harris make a video out of this deal.

First they ban your free speech, and now they're banning your stock purchases. They are telling everyday Americans these things; they literally did it just twelve hours after GameStop stocks soared. You and I and everybody else that we normally work with every single day are not allowed to benefit from the system that has been set up for us by the corporate elitists with their corporate greed, and when we achieve some kind of financial windfall, we can be shut down or get booted off. It's a no-win scenario.

There is one thing that I'm excited about for you, the reader, because a lot of the things that I'm writing about are actually happening as I'm writing them. This is so you can know what's going on and not forget what is happening and what those people are trying to do to you, not just the American people as a whole, but you. They are literally saying that you, peasant American, are not allowed to make money by risking your money in the stock market. Millionaires and billionaires are allowed to do it, but not you. The second you start beating them, there's a problem and they have to shut you off. So you are essentially told to go find another sandbox in which to play.

The feds not only relish treating us like children when it comes to matters such as the stock market, they enjoy wrapping us around their finger when it comes to unemployment compensation. As of early 2021, newly inaugurated president Joe Biden was preparing to propose an expansion of unemployment compensation, yet another well-crafted move designed to keep us in line while feeding off the government's teat (not to be confused with "government's tweet"). This takes us back to almost everything we've touched on in this book; concepts such as individualism, exceptionalism, and the motivation to work and be better than we currently are. We are flushing it away as a society.

Unemployment compensation used to be for people who were fired or let go, or their job went away and things like that. Unemployment compensation was never meant to be long term, let alone permanent. It was supposed to be a way to bridge the gap long enough for unemployed workers to find another job. Most people don't want to hear this, but the vast majority of folks who deserve to have jobs and who have done a good job at work and have a good work history can find another job in about thirty days, maybe sixty. That's because they apply the same work ethic to their career transition and job searching that they invested in the job they just lost. It might not be the job you love or your dream job, but if there is a job out there that you can do and for which you have the right skill set, you should grab it. There are almost always a lot of jobs out there. The problem is that there are people who don't want jobs, even if there are available ones that fit them.

They want someone to take care of them, and if it involves a free handout from the government, all the better. Easy Street.

As I write this in early 2021, at a time when covid-19 is still putting a significant damper in our lives and the workplace, Joe Biden has now made it so that if you fear covid-19 in your workplace, you can refuse employment based on that fear and draw unemployment benefits, which have never been higher. In addition to the regular unemployment check, which can run something like $275 to $300 a week, you can collect another pile of cash running into the hundreds of dollars weekly as part of the multitrillion-dollar covid-19 stimulus packages. How's that for a work incentive? A whole new form of equal opportunity.

What type of insane, crazy, absolute Looney Tunes, unicorn-believing fairy tale do we live in? Over the last year or so, some waiters and waitresses have been making more money on unemployment than they were when working in the restaurant business. Who wouldn't take that deal? Oh, I'm afraid of getting covid, so I'm just going to stay home and collect unemployment, which is going to be low enough for me to qualify for Medicaid. Then I'm going to qualify for a free phone because I don't make enough money, then I'm going to qualify for free Internet because the Internet is a human right now.

Every single thing that we're doing is disincentivizing, and I don't even know if that's a word. Deincentivizing people to actually get off of their sorry, Cheetos-eating-on-the-couch butt to go back to work. Go to work? "I don't feel good. I can't come into work today." What? Whaaattt? Back in the day, that wasn't an excuse. Who gives a crap if you don't feel well? Go to work. Are you dying? No. Then guess what: you're going to work. I mean, it's just the way it was.

My grandmother was the toughest woman I've ever known in my life. That woman would be on the verge of death, and she'd go to the post office and she'd run that mail route all day, every day because in those days, people went to work. That's what you do. You go to work. You start at the bottom, and you work your way up. It's not "I started from the bottom, and I automatically got here." It's "I started at the bottom, and now I'm here." See what I'm saying?

I was on active duty in the army for twelve years. After twelve years of that, after taxes, I was making only fifty grand a year. I mean, twelve years of daily activity, occasional missions, and being alert and poised to be in action 24/7. Don't talk to me about being unable to work. That tells me you are unwilling to work, unless, of course, you have some sort of medical issue or disability that keeps you at home, unable to perform whatever work specialty you have.

This is another thing that's wrong with society. People see people who are successful, and they tear them down because they are not. Sometimes that other person they see is me, although what they don't realize is that I get, on average, maybe five hours of sleep a night. They don't realize that I work seven days a week. They don't realize that, on average, if sales are down in my multiple businesses, I personally have to pay my employees to make sure they still have a job. Different types of pressure and accountability go with the territory. What are you willing to do to put food on the table and keep the lights on at night?

Somebody asked me the other day, "What are you actually doing besides talking, besides bringing, you know, attention to the issues?" Well, first of all, there aren't enough people talking about the real issues. Second of all, what are you doing? You're probably just going about your business and if the world implodes, "Oh, well." Right? Then the world implodes. "Oh, well, it doesn't affect me. I'll figure something else out because the government will save me. The whole world died off, as far as the economy goes, then we'll all be on the same playing field anyway, so it doesn't matter." You know how many people actually believe that and live by it?

This also applies to taxes. As an American, you have to ask yourself, "Are taxes actually constitutional? Are taxes actually good?" Taxation without representation was a big thing during the Revolutionary War. It was "You shouldn't be able to tax people without a representative of the people you're taxing." But what do you do when the people who do represent you no longer understand what taxes actually do to or for the working class and the working economy?

It's great that you're a lawyer. I'm superhappy that we have a bunch of lawyers in Congress. It's fantastic when it comes to writing law, although I don't really understand why it matters when we have a Supreme Court whose job it is to match legal considerations to what is constitutional. It's great that we have all these lawyers, and then there's Rand Paul, who is a doctor. That's awesome. I like Rand Paul. And Ted Cruz—I love Ted Cruz. He's a lawyer. That's fantastic. But where are all the small-business owners and individual entrepreneurs who should be in Congress? They are the lifeblood of

American society; exactly the ones you want to be representing you in the House and Senate. Where are all those people? I'll tell you where they are. They're not there. And the reason why they are not there is because we have created a fake thing about who is supposed to be fit to run for office. Either you need to have a lot of money, or you have to have family members who are in government in some capacity or other, or you have to be a doctor or a lawyer.

This is what most people believe. But take a good look at the US Constitution or your state's constitution—look real closely now. Tell me where it says you have to be rich, connected, or a doctor or lawyer to run for and serve in Congress. Ain't none of that in there nowhere. What it will say is that you have to be a certain age, you have to be a US citizen, and you have to reside in whatever state you would represent in Congress. There are other rules and requirements specific to each state, so you would need to look those up. Each state is different. Like Texas; you have to have lived in Texas for at least five years. Florida doesn't give a crap if you lived there starting only yesterday. And who says you have to have a college degree? I'm talking about myself here. I didn't graduate from college. But I'm richer than most people I know because I've learned how to operate my own businesses. Right?

So are lawyers really the best people to represent the people, when at the end of the day what really matters is what matters to communities? Taxes are a big deal. Small business is probably a gigantic deal. Gun rights, freedom of religion, health care. Those are probably about as big as it gets when it comes to the things the average Americans care about. Most everyday Americans care about five to seven things. That's it. They couldn't care less where a new road is going to go relative to the county line or the natural forest and that sort of stuff. They do care about their money, their taxes, their faith, their guns, their freedom of speech, their freedom of religion. And that's probably it for 90 percent of Americans today. So where are the real people in Congress who are supposed to be the representatives of all these people? Where are they? Where are all the congressmen who are actually normal people?

We've created a false illusion that people have to act a certain way, they have to live a certain way, they have to have a certain amount of money, they have to have a certain amount of prestige, they have to have a certain amount of fame, connections, and so on, when what we really need are people in Congress who actually know how to do some of the stuff about which they're voting and creating laws. Like, "Hey, okay, fifteen dollars an hour sounds great, but, you know, have you actually owned a business? Do you know what that's going to do to the backbone of the American economy?" It's going to destroy it—the mom-and-pops, for example. And then you're going to have more monopoly issues than ever because of what's going to happen when the small businesses go out. Walmart, Amazon, Target—all those and others are going to swoop in. A lot of the issues are being tackled by people who represent us and look good on paper because they've got all this prestige and wealth (even those who claim they really aren't wealthy but are in fact wealthy when you place them next to their mostly middle-class constituencies). They're not people who understand what it actually takes to do these kinds of things. There are people in Congress right now who are trying to fight Big Tech who don't even know how to run their own social media accounts. And I'm not saying that as a joke. It's not a joke. Especially when the truth is that Big Tech right now is the biggest threat to our society.

Who better to fight against Big Tech in Congress than people who run and operate massive social media pages? You see what I'm saying?

I think it's great if you're a veteran and have a notion that you want to run for Congress. That is a very good quality to have in Congress because having served has taught you certain things about discipline and hard work and that there are no set hours. But I also think you have to have something else. I'm not necessarily saying that being a lawyer or a doctor is it. You could be the best heart surgeon in the world and suck as a people's peaceful representative.

Average Americans have no clue where their taxes are going. Also, the whole conversation about abortion came back up again when Biden signed an executive order saying that the United States is going to give aid to foreign countries that promote and execute abortions. Let me say it again for those of you who read my last book and know this about me: I am 100 percent unwavering in any way, shape, form, or fashion—under any circumstance—I am anti-abortion in whatever language you want to speak it. Horrible things happen to good people—I get it. But I also understand that rape and incest are involved in fewer than 1 percent of all abortions.

Here's a question I asked on my show earlier this year: "What do you think the breakdown is in America of how many Americans are actually pro-abortion? Really, like, pro-abortion?" What I heard back from some listeners was that they didn't like the term pro-abortion. They much prefer pro-choice. Well, pro-choice is de facto pro-abortion, right? That's what it is. You are pro-murder at that point. And the reaction was all over the place. I said, "I believe it's more like 90–10 in terms of being pro-life versus pro-abortion, when you use those terms as they should be used." Honesty. Transparency. Quit playing around with phony semantics. Like calling a liberal viewpoint progressive. That is false advertising. What's progressive (and what isn't) is in the eye of the beholder. I would unequivocally state that a lot of what liberals say they believe in (even if they don't believe it in their heart) is regressive, plain and simple.

Some people say the pro-life/pro-choice argument is 50–50. I don't believe it's really even close to that. I said, "You really think it's fifty-fifty?" The vast majority of people who are pro-abortion are Democrats. And the vast majority of those Democrats who believe in abortion are women, and the vast majority of those are under the age of forty. That 50–50 number quickly starts tilting toward 90–10 when you break it down like that, narrowing down the demographic step by step. So the vast majority of people who are pro-abortion in America are female Democratic voters under the age of forty. Does that constitute the majority of America? Not even close.

Then I said, "Okay, let's break it down even further just for a minute. Let's remove the emotional aspect that is the abortion topic and talk money for a minute." Because everybody cares about their money, right? So I asked, "What do you think the percentage is of Americans that are pro their taxes funding people's abortions?" And everybody was like "Oh, heck, no." And then I said, "Exactly right." I said, "I would venture to say ninety-nine percent of Americans are probably not pro their taxes going toward people choosing to get abortions."

Everybody has an opinion, right? Some people are like "I have no problem with that." I then come back with "Well, let's flip the example. Say, I, Graham Allen, decide to go to a bar, have a bunch of drinks, and then I decide to get into a car, turn the key, and put it in drive." And, by the way, the second you do that, you've committed a felony. The second you get into the car drunk and start the car, even if you don't move it, you're already in trouble. And then I take off. I get pulled over, and I get arrested for DUI. Are you saying that your taxes should have to be used for my defense to get the DUI scrubbed off my record because it's going to ruin my life, it's going to ruin my job, it's going to ruin my career, and I can't have a DUI right now? Do you hear how ridiculous that sounds when you say it like that? Well, now, just substitute "abortion" for "DUI" in that illustration. Are you still okay with having your tax dollars used to pay for abortions?

It's the same thing, the exact same thing. Ninety-nine percent of the people you choose to support with your tax dollars opened their legs and whatever you insert to make things happen was inserted. We're all adults here. We know how babies are made. And then they just decide that they don't want the repercussions of those decisions anymore. So the taxpayer should have to help them because you're poor and can't afford to pay for an abortion. So taxpayers should have to help them get rid of their bad decisions. Well, then, we should have to do that with everything. Then again, this is where pro-abortion folks use language to whitewash the situation, spouting statements such as "Well, it's for the woman's health." Which is total bunk, just an evasion. But it sounds good in a courtroom or on a political stump. We all know what's really going on here; in the vast majority of cases, it's about women who consensually get laid and get pregnant, and now they want to get rid of an unwanted baby at taxpayer expense. It's the American way. On top of that, the "woman's health" argument applies less than 1 percent of the time.

A large majority of women—the second that they see that actual little *living* person in there moving around—they go, "I can't. I can't do it." Why would abortion clinics not want you to see that? Because they don't make any money if you decide to keep your child. God designed women to have an instant attachment the second they hear the heartbeat, the second they see those little hands move around on the sonogram. It's instinct. It's chemical. It's primal. Abortion and Planned Parenthood are a racket. They are *anti* everything natural and pure in our world. To be blunt, they are evil and generations from now, people will look at us as barbarians for even having this discussion.

So then I get this: "Oh, Graham, how can you be pro-life and pro–death penalty? It's easy. Even the Bible backs me up on this. And they're like "You're a Christian, too. And you're for murdering people for committing a crime?" Yes, as a matter of fact, I am. And the Bible is actually very clear, essentially saying "Hey, if you screw up on Earth, you are subject to the earth's laws. And if the earth decides that you broke so many laws that you're not supposed to be there anymore, guess what?"

Do I believe that you can find Jesus on death row and still go to Heaven? Yeah, of course, I do. Absolutely. But here is something else to consider: a baby is completely innocent. It is the only thing in this world that is absolutely without judgment, without sin, without repercussion of choice, anything. It's the only thing in our society that can be said to be completely innocent. It hasn't made any wrong decisions in its life.

We, as people, make decisions. Every day. Some people make bad decisions that lead to their possibly having to be taken out because they're such a menace to society, absolute noncontributors that society is better off without. "Oh, Graham, that's so horrible." Okay, are you telling me that you think the world was better off with Charles Manson in it? He wasn't executed, he died in prison. But my point is, why are we spending anything on people like him to give them comfort and sustenance? Why are we spending our tax money feeding these people three square meals a day, letting them basically die of old age in prison, and some of them coming out with doctoral degrees when all is said and done? So when you tell me the system isn't rigged, I say, "Just look at fifteen dollars an hour, and look down the rabbit hole that awaits us."

Equality of outcome? Well, that depends on what the outcome is, right? At fifteen dollars an hour, it doesn't sound too good to me.

Part Four

THE RESILIENCE

Nine

THE PURSUIT OF HAPPINESS

The pursuit of happiness is not a
guarantee of happiness.

I f you want to know the basis of our government and the premise behind how our country should be run—a mission statement, if you will—a good place to look is in the Declaration of Independence. It includes the familiar phrase "We hold these truths to be self-evident, that all men are created equal, that they are endowed by their Creator with certain unalienable Rights, that among these are Life, Liberty and the pursuit of Happiness."

The language is very specific, and our Founding Fathers had a reason for everything they wrote. This includes the Declaration of Independence, the first draft of which was written mostly by Thomas Jefferson, later to become the third president of the United States. Jefferson's draft of the Constitution was then slightly edited by a "Committee of Five" that included himself as well as John Adams, Benjamin Franklin, Roger Sherman, and Robert Livingston.

Much of Jefferson's phrasing in this historical document, such as the "pursuit of happiness" clause, was inspired by the works of others. Among those influences were the renowned English philosopher and physician John Locke, generally considered one of history's most influential Enlightenment thinkers; and the planter and politician George Mason IV, a delegate to the Constitutional Convention of 1787—one of three delegates who, ironically, ended up not signing the Constitution.

Included among Mason's earlier contributions, such as the first and second articles of the Virginia Declaration of Rights, adopted by Virginia in 1776, was the following (note the similarity to what Jefferson wrote in the Declaration): "That all Men are by Nature equally free and independent, and have certain Inherent Rights, of which, when they enter into a state of Society, they cannot, by any Compact, deprive or divest their Posterity; namely, the Enjoyment of Life and Liberty, with the Means of acquiring and possessing Property, and pursuing and obtaining Happiness and Safety."

Just as they do with Bible scripture, many people misinterpret and distort parts of the Declaration of Independence or the Constitution to fit their own agenda of whatever "woke" statement they are trying to make today. That's a tricky proposition for even the most astute American historians because the Founding Fathers were anything but woke. The woke culture goes against everything this country was founded upon, but in 2021 it is gaining momentum, its disciples growing bolder and more vocal.

We are still the greatest nation in the world, but the shining light that our country emits is getting dimmer as we creep closer and closer to socialism. It's a concept that has destroyed other countries at a rate no one can truly fathom. Yet its acolytes continue to push and promote it as though it's the greatest thing since GPS or sliced bread—take your pick.

We are blessed to be Americans. Along with that grace we are confronted by a very clear and present danger—one that we must fight against. Good times create weak men and women, a plight America now grapples with. We have become contented seekers of pleasure, believing ourselves to be entitled to happiness, however elusive it might be. Those of us who feel so entitled misconstrue what the Declaration says about life, liberty, and the pursuit of happiness:

> We hold these truths to be self-evident, that all men are created equal, that they are endowed by their Creator with certain unalienable Rights, that among these are Life, Liberty and the pursuit of Happiness."

Every word and phrase of the American Declaration of Independence bears significance—they have great meaning and were painstakingly chosen by its authors. You've heard that phrase about life, liberty, and the pursuit of happiness dozens if not hundreds of times, even if you never took US history in school.

Let's backtrack a bit. If I were to ask you which one of these three unalienable rights you thought to be the most important, most likely you would say "life." This is a normal response, and it comes from not thinking about it too much. So let me ask you another question: What is life without liberty? *Liberty* is defined by Merriam-Webster as "the power to do as one pleases; freedom from physical restraint; freedom from arbitrary or despotic control; the positive enjoyment of various social, political, or economic rights and privileges; the power of choice."

Furthermore, what is life without the freedom to choose? What is life without being able to do what you want? Marry whom you want? Work where you want? Love whom you want to love or make the money you want to make? On the other hand, turn it around and ask: What is liberty without life? It's nothingness. Dead people or those who were never born have no need for liberty. That's evident. I find the last part—"the pursuit of happiness"—the most intriguing, important, and all-inclusive of the three.

I have found myself asking this question a lot: Why put that phrase in there? The pursuit of happiness? What did they really mean by it? What was the real reason for this? You can't find an actual definition for this one. One possible guess, found on the website Your Dictionary and likely embraced by socialists is "The pursuit of happiness is defined as a fundamental right mentioned in the Declaration of Independence to freely pursue joy and live life in a way that makes you happy, as long as you don't do anything illegal or violate the rights of others."

That's all wrong. We live under the false idea that just because we are Americans, we are entitled to do anything and everything we want without rules or repercussions. We believe that within the rules there are no rules. Why is socialism creeping into America? In part because of the Internet, which by its nature and existence suggests that the pursuit of happiness means to do whatever you want as long as it makes you happy. This is a dangerous mindset.

Our Founding Fathers were entrepreneurial by nature. They understood that for democracy to work, exceptionalism, individualism, and the *drive* to work for what you get would be necessary. Otherwise, there is no democracy. There's no way the Founding Fathers could have imagined that the country they created would eventually turn into a country full of citizens who expected and waited on the government to save them. A country in which the average parent believes a child is not "really" grown until well into his or her twenties, a generation that would rather sit on a couch, play video games, and receive the minimal amount of money needed to survive without abandoning the creature comforts that go with zero responsibility.

The words *pursuit of happiness* were written into the Declaration to remind citizens that although they have an opportunity to achieve happiness in America, they would have to *work for it every single day*! The Founders expected those who followed them, for generations to come, to be *real* Americans who would get up and go to work as a given. Be creative. Be innovative. Be competitive. Don't accept *no* for an answer. Work and work and work to make America not only a better

place for ourselves but for *one another*. In fact, in the beginning America was all about the many becoming one. *E pluribus unum*. Now it's about me, myself, and I, and herein lies
the real issue.

I've asked myself about this a lot over the years. That's
especially true now that I've started contemplating and
talking about concepts such as life, liberty, and the pursuit of
happiness. My speaking engagements often in front of thousands of pairs of ears attached to heads prepared to process,
dissect, and challenge anything I have to say, and it is a challenge that I always look forward to. Give it your best shot. It
keeps me on my toes and on my A-game.

I've talked about this thing—"life, liberty and the pursuit
of happiness"—with audience members and others, discussing why the Founding Fathers would, in the first place, put
something like that into the Declaration of Independence and
on top of that, place them in the order that they did. It's worth
talking about; perhaps a debate is in order. Let's hash this
thing out and flesh out the talking points involved, because
obviously it's important stuff.

Let me clarify my thought process. Just like the Bible, the
Declaration has to be read in a context of understanding. We
have to understand that the Founding Fathers were going
against every aspect, angle, and accomplishment of history
to include every precedent in the history of the entire world.
For the first time, the winners of a war decided to do the exact
opposite of what every other victor had done; they decided
not to have a King (George) Washington. They decided not to
establish authoritarian rule over the people they could have

herded and controlled however they wanted. Instead, there would be no form of dictatorship.

The Founding Fathers were the very first people on Earth ever to do something like this. In effect, they were saying "You know what, that's not the way it's supposed to be. We are supposed to give this power back to the people and let the people be the boss, and let the people govern themselves, the individual states versus the federal government, etc., etc." Eventually, via the writing and implementation of the Constitution, there would be an executive branch (the president), a legislative branch (Congress, consisting of the House of Representatives and the Senate), and a judicial branch (the Supreme Court); as Abraham Lincoln would put it seventy-six years later, "government of the people, by the people, for the people." Without the people, none of those positions in the government matters. The Founding Fathers wrote those words to define a new world and prescribe a new way of life that would eventually be adopted by many other nations later on. No other country has gotten it as right as we have. But I digress.

Still: Why write "the pursuit of happiness" instead of just "happiness"? Why say "life, liberty and the pursuit of happiness"? For one thing, the Founding Fathers were hard workers, unlike many of the self-serving opportunists occupying important seats of influence in and around Washington, DC, today. They were entrepreneurs; they firmly grasped the idea of hard work, innovation, and success built out of failure, all calling cards of the classic entrepreneur. They realized that even though they had just won a war, they were now going to have to build not merely a new city or a new state or province, but an entire nation of what had become known as "the United States of America." It was going to be a Herculean task.

They and the people to whom they had entrusted the tenets of the Constitution would not only have to be given guidance on what was at stake and what needed to be done, they would also have to be inspired and motivated. They would need to see that the benefits—the payoff—coming their way would not only be an end product unto themselves but also everything they would see and experience along the way toward what America would become. It would become a pursuit on an unprecedented grandiose scale. Sacrifices would have to be made. The people would derive happiness from the journey, a sense of achievement that had never been experienced by mankind, not on this large a scale at least.

There was no blueprint, nothing to go by, at least nothing like what the Founders had in mind. So, they began by asking "What are our rights as people?" The Founding Fathers believed in God and Judeo-Christian principles. They started writing predicated on the shared belief that all men are created equal and are endowed by their creator with certain unalienable rights. That among these are life, liberty, and the pursuit of happiness. Those things weren't already formally in place on paper, so they had to anticipate, some of which they never could have imagined up until then. Whatever they came up with and whatever they put down in ink would have to hold up for generations to come. It would have to promote and utilize ingenuity, exceptionalism, and individualism—man formed in the image of God, doing His thing.

This would be a nation of enterprise and competitive markets but with everyone willing to put in the work to be successful and perhaps even to amass a personal fortune, with no shackles in place to hold them back. In a word, capitalism, with its competitive spaces. Who can come up with an idea first and then be the first one across the finish line as champion of his or her domain or industry or product or service? Who can have the best pricing or the more effective distribution system? All of that was also laid out in the Constitution, much of it implied as opposed to verbatim.

Foundational to this would be an anticipation, an unbounded optimism that we would forever have the responsibility of being in charge of our own happiness. The spirit of America would be imbued with the proposition that all men are created equal under God—equal in the sense that although we are all different, we can stretch ourselves without state-mandated limits. We can strive to achieve something better in our lives, to attain excellence, to measure up to a set of standards and goals we set for ourselves, define for ourselves. All men are created equal. That means that no soul, no human being, is above any other. We're all entitled to live here. We're all entitled to these liberties, as Americans, but they come with individual responsibility—a concept ignored by many Americans in 2021. That includes the right of freedom of speech, the right to bear arms, the right to not speak at all if we so choose, and even the right to tell someone to "shut up," right, Joe Biden? We are all entitled to that.

At the same time, we were not—and are not—guaranteed happiness. There is nothing in the Constitution, there's nothing in the Bill of Rights, that says you as an American are guaranteed to be happy, only that you have a right to be that way. Nor is it the role or obligation of the government, your neighbor, your boss, or your fellow taxpayers to make you happy. You must do that for yourself, and that version of happiness—as decreed by the Founding Fathers—comes in the pursuit of whatever you choose in making a worthy contribution to our country and your community, all for the greater good. If you hold out your hands, waiting for someone to place happiness into them, you've come to the wrong place. That was the viewpoint of our Founders. Happiness by itself is not in there. Oh, you can try to cut and paste it into your version of the document, try to make it fit into whatever you are selling as being constitutional, as in "I am due happiness," but that con won't cut it. It's a lie, no matter how many times you hear or read about someone claiming it to be true.

We have forgotten that as Americans, we are charged to be contributing members of society to America. That's what is meant by *pursuit*, and the happiness that is referred to in the Declaration comes from being an active part of that pursuit. We have not only a shared destiny as a collective but also an obligation to do our part in helping to shape it, and that's what is most important in our exercising that right. You want this country for yourself? You have to earn it.

As a Christian, I believe in the predetermination by God of what it is that you're supposed to do, even though free will is still a part of that; we always have choices. I believe that God has a plan for all of us, but in the freedom of choice he gives us, either we can go left or we can go right. Add to that the fact that God has never done anything with anybody who chose to sit on his or her butt, pull unemployment, and do nothing. Some of the people in the Bible were not good people. Some of them were people who, once they were saved, changed their name because of what they had done and how bad they had been before—like Saul becoming Paul.

This gets us to where we are in America today. We have moved far away from what the Founding Fathers believed we would do with this great opportunity of a nation. This goes back to what I said earlier in this chapter about how many people would choose life over freedom or the pursuit of happiness. But, again, what is life without freedom? Take it a step farther: What is life without the ability to choose whether or not we want to go to work? In that vein, we have the right to choose either to be a contributing member of society or to be a deadbeat piece of crap. What we don't have the right to do is say, "Hey, I know I'm a lazy piece of garbage. But you have what I want, so therefore, you should give it to me because as an American, I am endowed by my Creator to be happy." That is not true at all. It is a blatantly false interpretation. Some people are promoting unity within our country, and it has become a really big thing, yet one without substance. It means that dissent and the acceptance of divergence among political points of view is on the way out, at least as long as Joe Biden (or whoever succeeds him before the final three years of his term are up) remains president.

I touch on this elsewhere in this book, but it deserves another look and a deeper dive. *Unity* is not part of our

Constitution as far as individuals go. In fact, civil discourse is central to being an American. That's the whole point. That's why we have political parties. That's why we have representatives. That's why we have senators to go and fight out the differences that we have as a country.

You cannot demand unity. If you demand unity and enforce it into existence, by its nature it becomes conformity, and conformity leads to a tyrannical government dictatorship. People do not unite around force. They do not unite around "Well, you know, now that we have a change in establishment, we're going to be able to unify and blah, blah, blah." No. People unite around ideals, around inspirational messages, and around individuals who carry messages they believe in. We have a country that is literally divided right now, pretty much 50–50, with half of the country fully believing we are a constitutionally based nation and the other believing that much of the Constitution is flawed, out of touch, and in need of an overhaul. What the latter have in mind are precepts and constructs that go all over the map and have very little to do with what defines America.

Another problem with American society right now is that we're emotional about everything; I'm talking mostly about the Left, including Nancy Pelosi, who always seems to be in a state of barely controlled rage and confusion. The speaker of the House, no less.

America, what a country.

You can't have it both ways. You cannot run a country on emotion alongside constitutional principles, no matter how much you hate Donald Trump, whose biggest "crime" to date remains beating Hillary Clinton in the 2016 Electoral College (one of the few remaining colleges in America not run by nutty liberal administrators and professors).

Americans have life, liberty, and the pursuit of happiness bestowed upon them. It doesn't matter how much I hate Colin Kaepernick. He has just as much a right to play the victim card and race-bait America into making him a millionaire (thanks in large part to Nike) because he has the right to enjoy the pursuit of happiness and go after it and do whatever he thinks he needs to do to be happy as long as it does not impinge upon other individuals. It doesn't matter how much we don't like each other. What matters is that we all understand and we all agree that underneath that beautiful Declaration of Independence and the Constitution and the Bill of Rights is the fact that we're Americans and we're all entitled to these things. The problem is, we are confused about what we're actually entitled to.

The pursuit of happiness is not asking the government, "Please help me and give me a handout of happiness." The pursuit of happiness as envisioned by our founders is not "Can I please pull Social Security early?" or "Can I pull unemployment because I don't feel like working?" or "I'm scared of covid so I don't want to go to work anymore?" That's not the pursuit of happiness. Pursuit of happiness comes with a lot of work. Ashton Kutcher, the actor, who is also a very successful entrepreneur, once made a really powerful statement, saying "You know, opportunity looks a lot like hard work." It's true. Opportunity very seldom, if ever, comes with no work attached to it.

Kutcher is successful in business because he keeps an end in mind and works his butt off to achieve it. That's the issue we have: there is a generation of Americans who believe that everything that successful people have created for themselves should also be theirs. This falls into the category of "Equality doesn't always equal being equal," which I talked about in an earlier chapter. If you want what other people have, be better at what you do. You want to make a hundred grand a year? Be better. Or come up with an idea that somebody else hasn't come up with and make that idea a reality. You want to be better? You want to be a millionaire? Cool. Work harder and/or smarter than everybody else.

Yeah, there are people that are better than you—I can vouch for that in my own life. This is a bigger issue that begins with our parents and home life. Children are not being taught the truth, which is that they're not going to be good at everything. In fact, you're probably going to suck at most things, and you're going to be good at only a handful of things. That's the truth. That's how the real world works. If you can't teach your kids that truth, then as a parent you fail them. You are creating an entitlement mindset in your children. Collectively, we are failing our future generations by making them believe that they are entitled to everything they want. The truth is that the only thing they're entitled to is the *opportunity to try* to get everything they want. That's it. What ends up happening is people now believing they get passed over for promotions because they're black or because they're women or because they're this or they're that. Maybe you just suck at your job, or maybe somebody else is just better than you. Or both.

When I was in the military, I used to have a problem with the promotion standards because I was never the fastest runner. But I was good at everything else. Every single time, if somebody was a better runner than I was and had a higher PT score than I did, even though we matched up on everything else, he would be pushed ahead of me on the promotion list. That's because even though I had the same characteristics and qualifications as he did, he was better at that one thing than I was. So I would be passed over. Real life, man.

It's just the way the world works. Unfortunately, in today's day and age, many people misconstrue their rights as Americans. For one thing, your rights as an American don't trump my rights as an American. We all have the right to try. You create a business, cool. I have just as much right to create a business and potentially take you out of business. That's just the way it works. There are people who would view that as an attack, saying "Well, they're only doing that because I'm a minority," or "He's only doing that because I'm from the South," or "This is happening because I'm not a Christian." Spare me. Are you sure that's what's happening, or could it possibly be because you have a tainted history? Is it because you don't have the necessary certifications to work a certain job? Is it because you didn't study hard enough in school, and the other person had better grades and a 4.0 whereas you had a 3.7? Who knows?

I say again: one problem in today's world is that people misinterpret the Constitution and the Declaration of Independence, just as we misinterpret the Bible. The worst of these are Christians. They love to take bits and pieces of the

Bible—mostly out of context—and piece them together to make a point that, in truth, usually is not biblical. My favorite are folks on the Left who claim to be Christian but never go to church on Sunday (or Saturday) or attend a weeknight Bible study, yet they pose as biblical authorities and twist Scripture to claim falsely, for example, that acts such as adultery and homosexuality are not sin in the eyes of Jesus. Like the adulterous woman in the Book of John, who is confronted by Jesus who tells her she is not to be condemned. The part these phony Bible do-gooders conveniently leave out is Jesus in His very next breath telling the woman to "Go and sin no more."

There's all kinds of this stuff where people leave out key passages or text to suit their purpose. It's a similar deal with people who are critical of tattoos, quoting Leviticus to support their premise that all tattoos are immoral, when in fact that's not what Leviticus is saying. Leviticus 19:28 states, "Ye shall not make any cuttings in your flesh for the dead, nor print any marks upon you; I am the Lord." You must remember, this is Old Testament text easily misconstrued by twenty-first-century biblical watercooler congregants. They fail to grasp that the reference to "cuttings in your flesh for the dead" in those days (far preceding the life of Christ) referred to making cuts in the skin to honor dead idols or false gods. A tattoo of palm trees swaying in the wind or of a heart figure devoted to "Mom" certainly doesn't fit into that category. And any belief that Jesus was a socialist, well, don't even get me started on that.

Okay, too late—I got started. Now I'll finish that thought. In fact, Jesus was the opposite of a socialist because he talked about rendering unto Caesar what was Caesar's (taxation). Socialism, on the other hand, is the government demanding that you give your money to everybody else—spread the wealth, so to speak. Christianity is the exact opposite. Christianity is all about sacrificing and giving gifts to other people after you've given your time to God. Chalk it up as part of the pursuit. That's charity or generosity, *not* socialism. To this day, America is the most charitable country in the world. And this is based on Christianity. But guess what; if you don't work hard and if you don't pursue your own happiness, guess what you won't have. You won't have enough money to be charitable in the first place.

There is a large segment of Americans who not only want to revise Christianity to fit their false narratives or even remove it from public forums entirely but also want to write history that says our Founding Fathers didn't depend heavily on the Bible and Judeo-Christian precepts when writing the Constitution. This is not about righting a wrong; it's about whitewashing American history at a time when history textbooks for public schools are being rewritten to support liberal falsehoods. They are making great progress.

Today's liberal naysayers say this about the men who wrote the Declaration of Independence and the Constitution: "They weren't talking about God. They weren't talking about Jesus. They weren't talking about either New Testament or Old Testament principles." They're winning the argument to take God, the Bible, and scripture out of the roots of the Constitution. Either they'll say, "That's not what the Founding Fathers were saying," or they will even go for lower-hanging fruit, saying "Well, things have changed, and what was written into the Constitution more than two hundred years ago is outdated and doesn't apply anymore."

These people are relentless.

They are the same people who don't have any clue what actual racism is or what it's like to be really poor and actually go without food during a depression. People are realizing that the Founding Fathers were not angels. They were flawed; some were slave owners, but because they believed in Jesus and had a love of God, they were able to accomplish the most miraculous story and construct a shining beacon light for humanity. It was a light brighter than any that had ever been created before. When the Founding Fathers were writing the Constitution, they were already talking about how to get rid of the stain known as slavery. What many Americans forget is that slavery is a stain on our society that will always be with us. It happened, and we can't change it or undo it. However, people forget that the settlers were coming from an area where slavery existed. It has been that way throughout time, and even today, slavery is rampant in other parts of the world.

America proved that it was able to turn things around and in the right direction; it's no wonder other peoples in other countries have followed its example ever since. Those who founded America knew of the sins of their forefathers, and something clicked among them so that they essentially said, "You know what, this isn't right. This isn't the way it's supposed to be. We cannot say that all men are created equal and then exclude other people. We can't do that." This wasn't a deal where all of a sudden, they had an epiphany moment. Those men were old by the time that was going on. Well, not that old at the start of the Revolutionary War but old by the time the Constitution was ratified more than a decade later. It was all they knew. God operated through the Founding Fathers and through Abraham Lincoln and other great statesmen. Argue against that all you want. You'd be wrong.

Context is everything. People forget about that. People like to Monday-morning quarterback things like this, say what they would have done if such-and-such had happened, or what so-and-so should have done in such-and-such a circumstance. Twenty-twenty hindsight "expertise." Everyone who wants to dictate or second-guess what the Founding Fathers did or what Abraham Lincoln did or what John F. Kennedy did, or what Ronald Reagan did, if they had done any of that, there would be no America today. That's because every one of them would cower if put into any of those men's shoes at the most pivotal moments of their presidencies. They would not stand firm because they would have nothing foundationally guiding them.

The Founding Fathers were facing the worst of times. They literally made a decision to sign a piece of paper that, if they were wrong and they lost, they would be dead. Even in the face of sure death against the greatest army the world had ever known, the Founding Fathers created a foundational document that, though not perfect, was the most perfect one that had ever been created. They even knew that they couldn't think of everything. So they gave us the power to add amendments. To have the foresight and presence of mind to realize that they were not perfect and therefore the document that could be augmented was pure genius. Only in America.

I believe that the greatest mistake we ever made was Prohibition; we took away a right and a freedom. Later we changed the amendment and gave back the right. I am pro-amendment all day long. You want to add to rights and freedoms for Americans, add as many amendments as you want to. We can be at 337 amendments by the time it's all over with, as long as they add to or expand freedoms. But if we ever get into a conversation about taking away a right or a freedom, we're headed down the wrong road.

Back to the pursuit of happiness. The Founding Fathers were specific in their language for a reason. And they used a lot of other writings as reference, such as those of Locke and Mason. Thomas Jefferson referenced the Bible a lot in writing the Constitution. I often get mail from listeners of my show; some of it is fan mail, some of it is something else—and some of that something else is good, some not so good. Normally, I don't respond personally, but I will read some of it on the air and then discuss it.

One particular letter I got I thought would fit well into this chapter about the pursuit of happiness. This guy's letter started off with "You know, love your show, bro," and I thought, *Hey, this might be a pretty good email.* Then it said, "But can you tone it down on the God stuff a little bit because not all of us believe in God." I don't usually write back, but on this one I was like "Oh, yes. I'm going to write back."

We had a respectful back-and-forth via email. Finally, I just said, "Well, let me ask you a question (actually a series of questions, boom, boom, boom). Do you believe in America? Do you believe in freedom? Do you believe in the Constitution? Do you believe in our Bill of Rights? Do you believe that America is the greatest country in the world? Do you believe in our sovereignty as a nation? Do you believe in the founding fathers? And do you believe that we are privy to life, liberty, and the pursuit of happiness?"

He said, "Absolutely. I'm a patriot."

And I said, "Well, any real patriot, and I hate to break it to you, my friend, but if you believe in those things, then you innately believe in God because all of those things are based around Judeo-Christian values. We would not have any of those things if it were not for men who believed in God."

If you believe in those things, there is a part of you that believes in God. Just like I talked about people who believe in nothing. There's a belief there; there has to be. Same thing. You can't say that you believe in America, you believe in America's values, you believe in the Constitution, you believe in the Bill of Rights, you believe in life, liberty, and the pursuit of happiness and that all men are created equal, but you don't believe in God. That's what our Founding Fathers wrote into the Constitution. Someone or something has created us equally—those are Judeo-Christian values, and those are Judeo-Christian beliefs. You cannot claim that you believe in those things and not tip your hat to the fact that those documents were written and created by believers in God. We are able to live the entitled, selfish life we live today because of the Judeo-Christian values espoused by Christian men.

I guess everyone has his or her own unique definition of happiness. I'm just thankful for the fact that our Founding Fathers went with it in the Constitution, and that brings me happiness.

Ten

UNCENSOR AMERICA

The censoring of Americans is the start of oppression within America.

A merica was created with the shared understanding that individual rights endowed by our Creator were something worth fighting for. More important, they were worth dying for. But that sentiment was not unanimous, so let's not romanticize the Revolutionary War or even the Civil War. Romanticizing anything is stupid because it's never as cut and dried as depicted in *The Patriot*, one of my favorite movies, starring Mel Gibson. The movie makes it look as though all the colonies wanted to fight for their freedom, but that wasn't true at all.

Even Mel Gibson's character, Benjamin Martin, didn't want any part of it; he was dragged into it. It was through his eldest son, Gabriel (played by Heath Ledger), who saw something and believed in something that Benjamin didn't see or believe in at first, that he was finally brought around. That's the most powerful part of the story; not the story of the Revolutionary War but the story of how a lot of people actually were brought into the cause and eventually took up arms to fight the British.

It wasn't one of those beautiful almost clichéd moments where everybody all at once decided to do so. No, it was a group of people who saw something that was wrong and believed in fighting back. Over time they got others to buy into what they were seeing and believing in and then joining them. What they saw was actually a vision—something not real, not there, something that couldn't yet be seen. They saw something that *could* be, and they all decided that it was a hill—a battle—they were willing to die for, something you don't see in this day and age. Nobody is willing to stand up for anything today, to fight for anything, to believe in anything. Not really.

Let's ask ourselves one basic question: Would the Founding Fathers be proud of the America that we are today? Would they be proud of what we've done? Would they be proud of the direction in which we are going? Would they be proud that there is a growing population and percentage of Americans that are okay with Democratic socialism? Would they be proud of the fact that we are no longer concerned about individualism and exceptionalism but more concerned about me, myself, and I, and what can the government give me?

To answer all this, we need to go back to the founding of America and think about the reasons for our becoming America in the first place. For one thing, we were tired of someone else telling us what to do, how we could do it, and when we could do it. Of course, I'm talking about the British.

Taxation was a big issue, but an even bigger one was faith and the freedom to practice it however we chose, not the way the king of England and Church of England said we should. We couldn't love whom we wanted to love, couldn't do what we wanted to do, couldn't worship however we wanted to worship, and on and on. We were even forced to buy certain things and then taxed on them superhigh. It was crazy. That was what led to the Boston Tea Party, among other events of rebellion of that period. For some, the fight for freedom from British rule was regarded as a religious crusade, as described by PBS, which added, "Jonathan Mayhew, the pastor of the West Church in Boston, gave moral sanction to the war by preaching that opposition to a tyrant, in this case the British occupiers, was a 'glorious' Christian duty."

Usually, everybody believes something until they have to put their money where their mouth is or put their well-being, even their life, on the line. The amazing thing about the Founding Fathers, where we came from as a nation, and how we were created, is that people were willing to die for something they felt was bigger than themselves. Just imagine how much different America would be if that level of selflessness were still evident.

Think about the people who stormed the beaches of Normandy during World War II. Think about the people who fought in the Civil War to end slavery and to keep our nation whole. Do you really think they would be proud of us, of where we are right this second? Do you really think we are headed in the right direction? Do you really think they would look at us with pride? Or do you think they would look at us with confusion?

Do you not see how everything is bigger than the Founders could have ever imagined it to be and it's now being ruined? Do you not see that by going this route of selfishness, every problem in America, every problem in life, goes back to the most basic realm of selfishness? It all comes from selfishness, every issue, every problem, every argument in government, every argument in politics, every argument with your marriage or your spouse.

"I deserve this" or "I need this" or "You're not doing what I need you to do," blah, blah, blah. Or "You're not passing the budget that I want." Or "You're not giving me this when I want that." It all boils down to the most basic level of selfishness, from the most fundamental level of society all the way up to the federal government.

I sometimes sit back and wonder: What would the Founding Fathers think of us right now? What would the Founding Fathers think about our having organizations that are not even in the government, that have no political power and were elected by no one, yet they have more power than the US government? They have the ability to silence the president of the United States. I'm talking about the Big Tech companies. Back to them in a bit.

We have an economic system that literally says when you can work and when you can't work or when you can buy a stock and when you can't buy a stock? Would that be what our Founding Fathers wanted America to be? Do you honestly think that we are headed in the right direction in that regard?

The biggest healing in our nation can't occur until we're able to have real discussions and real civil disagreements and real civil discourse that have long been a part of America. The United States is really a disgruntled family. It has always been a family that fights and bickers all the time. It used to be that if an outsider took a poke at one member of our family, we would all quickly band together and do something about it, all together. Like on 9/12/2001. We've lost that. We've lost the understanding that at the end of the day, we're all just Americans.

I've often spoken on my show about "how to steal America." Now I'm going to take a similar tack, only this time I'm going to explain "how to make America not America anymore." You do that by making people afraid to be Americans. How do you do that? Start with Americans being known around the world as arrogant, having a "We're better than you" attitude, and proclaiming for all to hear, "We are the greatest country in the world." We don't say things like that without a deep-with-in-our-soul belief that we are indeed the greatest. We are the greatest. We are the greatest country there has ever been. So I ask again, How do you make America not America anymore? You make it wrong to be proud to be an American.

The biggest internal threat in America today is censorship—also better known as cancel culture. Censorship is taking away one of our fundamental rights as Americans, which is free speech, and not just the kind of free speech spelled out in the First Amendment—the kind that is protected from governmental interference or limitations. I'm talking about the kind of free speech that is pervasive in everyday life, such as the kind that might get you knocked off Twitter or banished to the hinterlands by Mark Zuckerberg and his Facebook police.

Free speech is what makes the world go round. We've already talked about the fact that divisiveness and division are actually good things—not to be feared or written off as dysfunctional. Well, you can't have division, and then you can't have dialogue to fix that division if you don't have free speech or the freedom to argue with people—or the freedom to call someone a derogatory word that you probably shouldn't have called him or her. That doesn't make it the right thing to do, but you have the right to do it.

We now live in a world where cartoon characters are canceled because they're offensive or called something like "inappropriate," when even a fifth grader knows that what is inappropriate to one set of ears is fine to another. Now any cartoonish depiction of, say, a dog in a policeman's uniform is verboten because of the George Floyd incident. Then there is the Pepé Le Pew character, a cartoon skunk who appeared in the first *Space Jam* movie with Michael Jordan. Pepé was cut from the sequel, starring LeBron James, after the *New York Times* ran a piece condemning Pepé for promoting the rape culture. Scenes in Disney movies are being cut because they're viewed as misogynistic. Six Dr. Seuss books are no longer being published because they contain racist elements. You can't buy Aunt Jemima pancake syrup anymore. Curious George books have been panned by critics for daring to show a white man bringing home a monkey from Africa. The portrayals of Native Americans in her "Little House on the Prairie" novels have been criticized so often that Laura Ingalls Wilder's name was in 2018 removed from a lifetime achievement award given out by the American Library Association.

Meanwhile, one of the most popular songs in America over the last year or so was about a wet vagina (Cardi B's "WAP"), but that is acceptable? Apparently. And that is completely acceptable. There is Kevin Hart, who in 2018 pulled out of hosting the following year's Oscar ceremony over the backlash that was created when someone dug up some gay-themed tweets and jokes of his—from nearly ten years earlier! So Hart can't host the Oscars, but Cardi B can be shown having sex with another woman on a bed on a stage for a Grammys show that is globally televised. There's a lot wrong with this picture, folks. In fact, if you say anything about pop culture or the Left or the music industry or Hollywood in general, you're a conspiracy theorist, or you're a hate speech person, or you're a bigot, or you're this, or you're that.

Seriously, I'd like to know who is in charge of all this sort of stuff, canceling culture right and left, even because of stuff that happened a decade or more ago. Who's behind this? Who's in charge of this? Stand up and be counted, whoever you are. It's as though there's some evil force pulling the strings on this, and the Left just seems to go along with it.

Do I believe that the vast majority of Americans have a problem with Dr. Seuss but they don't have a problem with their children seeing a woman talk about her wet vagina on a televised awards show? No, I don't believe that to be true. I saw a viral TikTok video of a woman who had an infant who could not have been more than six months old, declaring that her baby was gay and that was going to be great. Why? Why did that woman do that? I don't think for a second she really believes that to be true. She just knows that if she says something outrageous like that on TikTok, she'll get a lot of views and she'll be TikTok famous. And that is completely acceptable. But for somebody to go online and simply say, "Hey, you know, maybe we should have other conversations about this whole coronavirus thing," or "Hey, you know that Joe Biden, in fact, violated mathematical law in 'winning' the 2020 election. Shouldn't that be something that we should at least have a conversation about?" Canceled. Censored. You cannot say these things.

I saw a fact-check that showed that since Joe Biden had taken office, gas prices had begun to soar. One gas station in Santa Monica, California, was selling gas at just under six dollars a gallon within the first sixty days of Joe Biden's term in office. After that post was fact-checked, I click on the fact-check, and it said, "Missing context." So I click on it, I'm like "Oh, well, this person must have made this up or it's a photo from, like, during Katrina or whatever. The fact-check said, "This gas station is known to charge more than other gas stations. The average gas price has only risen by forty-three cents a gallon in the first six days of Joe Biden's term." So in my interpretation, the fact-check was really saying "Yes, this is a real gas station that is really charging these gas prices, but because that makes us look bad, we're going to say that this is now missing context because we just feel like it."

I put out a tweet that said that the $1.9 trillion covid relief stimulus package approved in March 2021 was going to cost the average American about $5,700, and only some Americans were going to get $1,400 in stimulus funds. Well, I got fact-checked for that, for which I had to issue a correction. This is what I was forced to say as a correction: "Economists say the cost of the plan cannot be attributed to every American in this way, though they differ on the specifics of what its impact actually would be." In so many words, the fact-check was "We actually don't know if you're right or wrong, but because we don't know if you're right or wrong, we're automatically going to say you're wrong as a default because it's Graham Allen, and that's what we're going to do."

That is the world we live in. And society cannot function this way. Cancel culture is the symptom of what is taking place in America in regard to censorship. Cancel culture is what happens when you allow things like censorship to creep in unchecked. It's a free-for-all in which politically correct people of influence, apparently arbitrarily decide what is offensive or hurtful or whatever other vague term you want to use to describe it and get you to cease and desist. Not only that, then have to apologize for it.

Somewhere in the shadows or behind a giant curtain there is someone pulling the strings on all this; there has to be. They are getting away with it while having a jolly time, I'm sure. They might be part of the Deep State running this country, many of them nonelected and content to stay hidden. Show me any good, honorable society, any good, honorable *country*, in which the people who were hiding newspaper articles from

Twitter, restricting what you could say or restricting what you could do, trying to push gun control laws, or any one of a number of other things—show me the societies that actually had the best interests of the people in mind. The answer is, there aren't any. We have to free ourselves from allowing this to happen.

Our government has failed us. That is the truth. Our elected officials have failed us. That's right. Your precious congressman who's been in office for ten terms—guess what? He or she is failing you because he or she is not prepared to fight the greatest threat to Americans right now. The greatest threat facing Americans every day is censorship. If you're reading this book and you're in your seventies or eighties or older, maybe it doesn't affect you. But it affects your kids, it affects your grandkids, it affects your great-grandkids. That's because the predominant manner in which we communicate with each other is online.

Those of you reading this book are part of the 10 percent of the people who listen to me online who have bought or will buy this book. Now, I would love to be able to say that 100 percent of the people who watch me online or on TV bought my book, but that's just not the way the world operates. Again, I say, the primary way we communicate is online. And the way that we're communicating online is tainted, it's governed, it's watched, and it's censored. We're not allowed to say anything that goes against the establishment.

Worse yet, we're no longer just fact-checking the news to see if what somebody reported is factually wrong. We are now fact-checking opinions. *Opinions.* We're not even allowed to have an opinion anymore in America. Like if I were to say, "I believe Joe Biden is doing a poor job of running this country" (although, in real life, I don't believe he is actually the one running it). That's giving my opinion, and if I were to say that online, I know with some certainty that I would be fact-checked, even though it's an opinion. "I like the color blue." Fact-check. "My favorite football team is the Alabama Crimson Tide." Fact-check. "That's a very nice jacket you are wearing, ma'am." Fact-check, and while we're at it, #MeToo, too.

We have to stand up to this nonsense. We cannot allow this to be. We have to fight back against this because *noncensorship* (freedom of speech and expression) is actually a bedrock principle of what America is supposed to be about. Imagine if Facebook had been around back during the Revolutionary War and John Adams, Benjamin Franklin, and Thomas Jefferson and all those people started having these conversations online: "Well, you know, Britain is actually, you know, taxing us without representation." They would have been fact-checked for saying that. No question. Thomas Edison might type in something like "You know what? I really think that I can create a candle that will last forever." He'd be fact-checked, and the fact-check would say, "That's not true. There is no such thing. There's no candle that can last forever. This man is spreading conspiracy theories. He's spreading lies." Or how about Jonas Salk taking to Twitter to report, "I have found a vaccine for polio." Here's what the fact-checker might write: "No, he didn't. There is no vaccine for polio. Hide in your houses and fear for the rest of your lives."

Everything is fair game for the cancel culturists. Every-thing. These are evil people, without question.

A lot of people like to forget that during the days of slavery in the nineteenth century, it was the Democrats who wanted to *keep* slavery. Now, a lot of people will argue that the Demo-crats back then are the Republicans of today, and Republicans will argue that that is not the case, it is the exact opposite. But the fact of the matter is this: the party that did not want slav-ery to end during the slavery days was the Democratic Party.

The danger we live in today is such that it doesn't matter what you say; in most cases, no one cares. However, it *does* matter what you say in terms of the harm that can come your way if you say the "wrong" thing. If you say anything that is the opposite of what the news tells you is true, you are auto-matically deemed a liar. You're immediately told that your voice and your opinion no longer matter and your voice and your opinion do not deserve to be heard by other people. Does that sound like a free society to you? This is how society works in China. Oh, wait—you want to cut China some slack, give them a break, show pity for them because most everyone else in the world blames them for the coronavirus/covid-19 (as they probably should)? If that's what you believe, you need to unbury your head from the dirt and get back into the game of life.

A discussion about censorship in America today has to include the world of social media. For such a supposedly free and open forum for communication that virtually connects the world, Facebook takes the cake for shutting down voices it doesn't tolerate. Actually, Facebook might be tied with Twitter for the top spot in the shutting down of American free speech, but you get my drift.

The deal is that for some time now, Facebook has been using a scoring system to give social credit to people. A rating, if you will. Are you "good" or are you "bad"? Credits are good, and dings are bad. That's right, you can get dings on your Facebook account; get too many, and you're blocked from using your account anymore. Big Brother is watching, and his name is Mark Zuckerberg. Once you get ding-a-linged, you're not allowed to speak, you're not allowed to be seen, and you're not allowed to be heard—unless you fall back into line.

The censoring of Americans is the start of oppression within America. Think about it for a second. In his first address after becoming president in January 2021, President Joe Biden told the American people, and I'm paraphrasing here, that "as long as you do what we want you to do and we can get three million vaccinations a day, you might be able to gather in small groups for the Fourth of July." Think about the irony of a sitting US president telling free Americans what they are free to do on Independence Day. It not only shows how far we've fallen, it shows how far the government has fallen away from the people. It further shows that when Joe Biden speaks nowadays, he probably doesn't really know what's coming out of his mouth much of the time. He's just a talking head for whomever is pulling his strings and whispering into his ear. That was clearly evident on March 25 when he finally gave his first official press conference from the White House (more than two months after his inauguration), in which he said a lot of nothing for sixty-two minutes and either droned on saying stuff filled with blatant inaccuracies—like citing stats about the southern border chaos that were way off the mark. He spent much of his time reading talking point "cheat sheets" his staffers had prepared to help him answer questions from reporters. It wasn't just a sad sight, it was a disturbing one: the president of the United States, clueless and befuddled.

We need a revolution in this country. Not just a biblical revolution, either, although we've talked about that many times. The church is just as much to blame as the government is for where we are in America today. We need a *government* revolution. To be blunt, anyone who is sixty years or older needs to be immediately kicked out of Congress because they no longer understand the actual threats against our country, and some of the worst threats are coming from within. The only exceptions would be anyone sixty and older who can convince his or her constituents that he or she is fully up to speed on the nuts and bolts of what is going on in the world of censorship and cancel culture and understands the technology involved. Maybe it's not their fault, but anyone who flunks this test is *out.*

If you spend twenty or thirty years or more on Capitol Hill, how can you relate to normal Americans anymore? And yes, I'm asking you, the reader, that question. Think about this: if you spend ten years on Capitol Hill, how are you a normal American—someone who understands what normal Americans are actually going through and what they need and want? We need term limits. But if you talk about term limits, you get into trouble. You're not allowed to talk about term limits. How dare you? Career politicians and wannabe careerists believe that once they are settled in to their office, "We should be able to stay here until we die and make millions of dollars because we have insider trading knowledge, we know all this and that. No, I'm all about capitalism."

We need a revolution in this country because we have people in Congress right now—I estimate 70 percent—who are fifty and older. That includes both the House and the Senate. I don't know those to be exact numbers, but just based on what I see on TV, its a solid guesstimate. Most of those people don't even have any clue how to log in to Facebook. They have no idea what's actually going on with social media in general, and they have no idea how to combat it. They might be good people, but you can be a good person and still be the wrong person to defend and fight for the rights and freedoms of the people you represent in the district and the state in which you reside.

We need fighters in America. We need fearless people to charge out there, stand strong, and be willing to take a few arrows in the back defending the people back home. We need people with the discernment to understand that not only is our way of life being threatened but our way of thinking as well. We're being made to believe that we're more divided than we really are. I've already talked about division as a good thing, but anti-American progressives want you to believe that it's always a bad thing. I've also talked about how equality of opportunity and the way we are viewed by God are great things, but equality of outcome is bad. They want you to believe that everybody should have the same stuff and live in the same house and have the same job and make the same money. That way of thinking says that on your first day on the job you should be making just as much money as the CEO. But where is the incentive to become the CEO?

In such a world—and we are headed in that direction—why would anyone in his or her right mind want to go to school for ten years or however long it takes to be a doctor, only to end up making the same amount of money as someone who dropped out of school for good at age twelve and is now working some menial task that doesn't require a high school diploma? But if you say something like that on social media—essentially, criticize socialism—you get censored, you ding-a-ling. Worst of all, and I do mean worst of all, if you say something that enough people hear and they don't like, you get canceled. Your family is ruined. Your job is ruined. Your life is ruined. Your way of life is ruined, just like what happened to Will Smith's character in the movie *Enemy of the State* that came out more than twenty years ago. Smith's character unwittingly stepped on the toes of part of Deep State America, and it cooked his goose but good. He lost his wife, lost his family, lost all his assets, all his credit cards canceled—a total mess.

Who would have ever thought that Americans would turn on other Americans so much that even though you just said something that I don't particularly like, I want to ruin your *entire life*? Not because you said something bad about me but because you said something bad, say, about Taylor Swift. "And because Tay Tay is my favorite person in the world and you said something bad about her, we're coming for everything you've got. We're finding out everything about you. We're going to ruin your life. We're going to tell your wife or your husband that you had affairs, that you cheated on your marriage."

It's a cruel world out there, and it's getting nastier, by the way.

As much as I hate to say it because I disagree with him politically, everybody needs to be a little more like Eminem. Yes, *Eminem*. Bear with me here. Eminem has been trying to be canceled for the past twenty years—it's part of his renegade-like persona. Even the US government at one point tried to stop Eminem from making records. But the people at TikTok have found one of his lyrics to be offensive toward women, so they tried to have him canceled.

What did Eminem do? Well, he *didn't* do what Chris Harrison from *The Bachelor* did and cave in by dragging himself to race education training as he was told and stepping back from his job and all that other kind of stuff, along the way issuing apologies and essentially bowing to the cancel culture mob. I don't know, there might have been a few tears involved. Eminem took a different path, a bold one. He literally made a song that told everybody to go get bent, that he did not care, that "If you wanna cancel me, I couldn't care less."

Tucker Carlson with Fox News, the same thing, made a simple statement that the military is catering to woke culture and it's hurting the military overall. So what happened? High-ranking military folks in uniform went after a private citizen—Carlson—because they didn't like his personal opinion that he spoke as a free citizen, a journalist on top of that.

That is scary enough by itself—having the military come after you. But what did Tucker Carlson do? He apologized to no one. He said he meant every word he said. He didn't take it back. You can love him or hate him; he said what he meant and meant what he said.

That's what we need. We need more people, especially people in Congress in leadership positions, to say, "You know what? I'm not sorry. I said exactly what I said, and that's what I meant. You can either vote me out or you can *shut up*." That's the way it goes. That's the way our democracy goes—or at least *should* go. The reason we are being censored, the reason cancel culture is running rampant, is that we have leaders who are more concerned about keeping their precious high-paying jobs with great bennies than they are about actually doing the job that they're supposed to be doing. If they were more concerned about supporting Americans, they would be willing to lose their congressional seat or Senate seat. They should ignore people's knee-jerk opinions and pay closer attention to what's right for the people they represent. The end; nothing else matters. But the problem is, we have people more concerned about becoming Insta famous or Facebook famous and running to become elected members of our government. We need real leaders to stand up.

I would fix the problems right now that would reset America. I say let it go. Let everybody say whatever they want to say. Go back to the way it used to be. You can call me whatever you want to call me, even if it's the most horrible thing ever. Say whatever you want to say as long as you don't incite violence or try to assassinate me. Otherwise, you have the right and the freedom to say whatever you want and do most anything you want to do, short of the exceptions I just mentioned.

You know what: you should feel free to go on Facebook right now, start a live feed, and tell the whole world that you know Santa Claus is real. Why? Because he's your pappy. And you know that Santa Claus is real because you see him every day; he had a hand in birthing you, and he's your dad. And I should have the right as a free American to watch that live feed and say one of two things: (A) "This is amazing. I now know who Santa Claus's daughter is," or (B) "This chick is insane." We should have the ability to do that as Americans. And then move on.

During the covid-19 outbreak, we should have had the ability to listen to doctors who had opinions different from Lord Fauci's, the Sith Lord of the fifth dimension in the NIH. We should have had the right and the opportunity to listen and decide for ourselves. Instead, the government told us what we could do, and we let it happen.

So how do we fix the problem? We need leaders. We need people to step up. We need to stop being afraid of what people think about us and more afraid about the crap we're leaving for our children. Our lives are written already. I'm thirty-four years old. I have no idea what comes next, but I know where the good Lord has put me now. And the good Lord has put me here to be a voice. I believe that everybody will face two judgments when they die. Whether you're a Christian or not, this is my Christian perspective worldview, and you're going hear it. I believe, first thing, that you're going to have to deal with "Did you know the Lord? Yes or no?" We all know what happens if you say no. But then, second, I think you're going to be judged on "What did you do with your life? What did you do with the opportunities you had? And what did you do with the opportunities I gave you?"

For some reason, I've been given a platform. I've been given an opportunity to have you read this book in the first place. Either you know who I am or you found it in Target or Walmart or wherever, and now you're reading it. My opportunity to stand up is now. And I don't care if I'm canceled tomorrow. I'm going to say what I want to say because it is what I believe and it is what I think and it is what I feel. We're fighting a war under the veil of politics in our country. And right now we're losing because too many people are ignoring the fact that we are actually *already* fighting the war.

We're fighting the war right now in America. Most people just don't know it yet. I liken it to when Americans wanted to ignore the advances of Nazi Germany in the 1930s, before World War II. We knew something horrible was going on. We knew something was happening underneath, and it was happening well beyond Germany. We ignored it until Pearl Harbor. Pearl Harbor happened, and then we could no longer ignore it anymore.

Here's the truth. Our Pearl Harbor moment here, still early in the twenty-first century, has not happened yet. There's a chance that the war has already started and we now need warriors to step up. We need people to come forward who are not afraid to speak the truth—not "their truth" but *the* truth. The truth is in the realm of America, the US Constitution. The truth is that the Constitution was formulated by people drawing on Judeo-Christian values for this to become a Christian nation. *This is a Christian land.*

Now, you don't have to be a Christian to live here, but, by God, those are the rules. And if you want to live here, you have to play by the rules here. That is what we abide by. If, however, you choose to step on this country's flag while burning it and think we'd be better off if we were more like China or Russia or North Korea or Iraq or fill in the blank, you are nuts. Go away—no one is stopping you, except maybe your heartbroken parents. Even though that gives people like me just cause to censor you for being an idiot, we acknowledge that you have every right to say it and believe it. In God we trust. We need leaders to stand up and help fight the battle that threatens to end America. How do you stop America from being America? You make Americans afraid to be Americans.

Look at what's going on right now. I believe that gun rights is going to be the straw that breaks the camel's back because the cancel culturists are already going after the First Amendment. Just within the last couple weeks here in March 2021, as I work on this chapter, there have been mass shootings in Atlanta and in Boulder, Colorado. Excuse the pun, but they have given Biden and the administration more ammunition to push toward tougher laws on gun ownership, and, who knows, they might be the opening the Democrats have long sought to revoke the Second Amendment and try to take away all our guns. Mass shootings are catnip to the anything-goes political agenda of progressives; each time one happens, it renews their obsession with getting rid of guns for everyone.

Joe Biden is already trying to pass gun laws and registrations. I don't know where it'll all be by the time this book comes out. I think the moment the government tries to say, "You no longer can have this, this being your guns," things will go very badly very quickly. And if we don't want our children and our children's children to have to deal with that, we need people to step up now, we need leaders to step up now, and we need warriors who are not afraid to take the first steps.

If you're sitting there and thinking how much you are in agreement with everything that I'm saying but you don't know what to do about it, I've got something to say to you: stop waiting on someone else to do it for you, because that's the problem. So many people say all the time, "You need to do this or somebody needs to do something," but then they look in the other direction for somebody else to do something. No. What we need is for people, just one person to start with, to actually do something. One person doing something becomes two people doing something, which then becomes four, which then becomes eight and sixteen and thirty-two and so on and so on and so on, until eventually there is a force so strong that nothing can stop it.

How do you "uncensor" America?

You simply let Americans be Americans.

Eleven

LIVE LIKE IT'S 9/12

Are you ready to join the battle to win back America?

I want to end this book by talking to you one on one—one to another—as just "Graham," not "Graham Allen, this figure everyone thinks that they know." Does that make sense? What I mean is that when you achieve a certain amount of notoriety—dare I call it *fame*—many people view you as something more than you really are. There is a scene in *"A Star Is Born"* where someone asks, "Why is it when you are famous everyone starts calling you by your first name?" That's what I mean. Just call me Graham. I'm nothing special. I'm just a person. I'm simply an American just like you.

Somehow over these last four years, I've become something more than just me. I've become this public figure people think they know. I didn't ask for it, but here we are nonetheless. I've become something that is impossible to maintain or keep up forever—I can't be "on" twenty-four hours a day, seven days a week. My weeks wear me down about as much as I can stand right now. I can't even begin to tell you how many people in the conservative fight with me are hurting, tired, or even sick. This battle takes its toll. It gets you on the back end, and no one can keep it forever or, worse, by themselves.

Others, perhaps you, are needed to join this battle to win back America before it sinks into oblivion, never to be heard of again, as is happening right now. I am not going to lie to you. So many people do. I realize that in this day and age we expect more lies than the truth. So I am going to tell you just that: the truth. This fight and this battle to win back our country is extremely hard, and I am right in the middle of it. Although I didn't ask for it initially. I kept going, knowing it would take a lot out of me—as it does to untold thousands of others—and I'm not superhuman. No one is, and we can't win this battle alone. Don't get me wrong; I'm having a great time and love what I do. I do it because I *believe* in America. I believe that what we have here is worth fighting for. I believe it is worth dying for.

This thing, and this gig, are really time consuming and soul crushing, so much so that it takes its toll on all of us. I can tell you that every single person I know in this movement is on some sort of anxiety meds, is dealing with depression, drinks caffeine by the bucket to keep going, and/or has developed medical issues due to stress. This is more than being famous. It is choosing to believe in something that matters more than yourself. We only have one life to live. What do you want your legacy to be? The time for thinking is over. It's time to act.

Here's the thing, and I'm not trying to sound any alarms. I know that I won't live forever. I have often joked that I will be lucky to see fifty. I say it jokingly, but it is mixed with truth. Like many men my age, I struggle with the ever-chasing demon that I don't have as much time as everyone else, so I'd better make the time I have count. There's a sense of urgency in which I struggle with having a purpose of meaning. I struggle with the *real* questions such as: Is this all worth it? Am I doing the right thing? Am I being the best husband, father, friend, owner, and patriot that I can be? And can I really balance all this, or is it a seesaw effect in which sometimes you are better at one thing than another and then those things switch with each other? I honestly don't know.

Here is what I do know: I'm just a man. Honestly, much of the time not the best one. I fail. I fall. I sin. I hurt. I fear. I destroy. I doubt. I'm just a person. I'm just like you. We are the same in that regard. I just choose to let everyone see it. I choose to not be afraid to let people see me fail. It doesn't mean that it doesn't haunt me to fail. Does that make sense? Good. Let's keep going.

There are so many people who desire something. They want something more than what they have. More power to them if they can actually identify what that something is; many people can't. All they know is that they want to make a mark or own a business instead of working for someone else. They want out of a bad situation but are waiting for the right time and the right place to make the leap. The truth is, there's never a right time and right place for anything great. No one ever accomplished anything by being comfortable. You just go for it. You jump. You move. You decide.

Christians will disagree with what I just said and say, "God will provide a way." Now, I am a Christian, and I do agree with that to an extent. But I believe it is wrong thinking to believe that God will open a door for you and push you through it, that everything is somehow going to work out without a lot of hard work and effort on your part. That is the prosperity gospel we often hear preached, and it is *wrong*! It is misleading and creates false expectations leading to severe disappointment when things don't turn out the way you wanted. What if God's manner of provision is giving you the gut feeling to jump, because he knows that's exactly what you need?

There are two types of beliefs in this world: the "top of the mountain" belief and the "first step" belief. Some people dream of what they want to accomplish. That's the top of the mountain. Others simply see the first step—like knowing you need to quit your job but having no clue what to do after that. Whatever your belief is, what you do with it and what comes afterward fall into the faith category, something that most people do not possess enough of. Do you *really* believe in your dream? Do you really believe in America? Do you really believe in your values and morals no matter what the personal cost? Are you fully committed to it? How's your faith? Many people will tell you what their dream is and what inspired them to formulate it, but what happens when push comes to shove? Many people claim to be a patriot or love God or guns, but what happens when they are challenged or, worse, people come for the things they claim to hold so dear? That's when you find out how *real* people actually are.

Americans today, in general, are weak in this regard. Without a moral compass attached to a belief, we walk through life like drones, destined only to accomplish what the system says we can accomplish. *I hate it!* I want you to see what I see. I want you to feel the passion and the determination and the desire that I feel to succeed. The faith that I have in America. The love I have for our freedoms and what they represent. I want you to remember who you are not only as a person but as an American. I want you to live your one life as though it is the *only* life you are going to get—because that's reality. There are dreamers with no follow-through: they are even more dangerous than people who are lazy. Dreamers start something, and then, when it turns into work, want no part of it. These people are what I call *fakers*. Again, anyone can say he or she believes in something, but when the going gets tough and the mission becomes a taxing grind, you quickly find out who the real players are.

Real players step up to the plate and put their necks on the line. In some cases, running for a public office with the sincere intent to win, get into office, and make things better, put your community, state, or country back on track, while getting rid of the waste and political garbage, is the way to go. If you don't like the decisions your local community representatives are making, then run for city council or mayor or governor, state house, or state senate. Run for Congress or president! *Just do something!* Consider this a call to action—*your* action.

If you think Congress is useless—and it is—then run or primary someone who is the problem, and take up the mantle to fight and fix it!

Americans today are scared. They're lazy. They make themselves useless by shying away from the rigors of fighting for anything that remotely matters. Everyone acts as though he or she believes in something. Everyone wants to claim that he or she is a patriot. Everyone wants to claim this and claim that. All talk, no cattle. Quit jabbering and talking big, and start taking action, even if you start small. I'm *not* saying to go storm the Capitol building. To this day and forevermore, I will disown and disavow the actions of January 6, 2021. They were about as dumb and cowardly and useless as it gets. From a military perspective, every single military person—active duty, retired, or just plain veteran—knows that sort of garbage is the stupidest thing that could have ever happened. There was no declaration of war. There was no plane with an intended purpose of resolve. They were a bunch of cowards at the end of the day, okay? All they did was take ten giant steps backward in fighting for what's best for our country. It was a trap, and we walked right into it.

It goes back to what I said earlier in the book: the Founding Fathers had no Plan B. You can't really commit to changing anything while carrying a Plan B in your pocket; that shows you don't have full confidence in Plan A. Big mistake. When the Founding Fathers signed the Declaration of Independence, they knew that if they did not win, they would be dead. It was as simple as that. That would be it. Over. Done. There was no reset button. There were no Plans

B, C, D, E, F, G. People nowadays want the whole alphabet in assurances.

Please listen to me. If you have a Plan B, you are destined to fail. Whether or not you know it, you are planning to fail. Think of it like a pull-up. If you believe you have done the max amount you *think* you are able to do and the drop to the ground is only two feet, you will probably let go of the bar instead of fighting for one or two more. Now take that two feet, and turn it into an abyss. Would you still let go? Would you be too tired to keep going? Or would you dig down a little deeper and find something within you to pull yourself up one more time to keep from dying? Of course you would. When you have no Plan B because Plan A is the only option, life actually becomes very simple. So why do you live your life with a "safety net" two-foot drop beneath you in all aspects of your life? Why do you allow bad decisions to be made in our country without finding the ability deep inside you to do something about it? We have safety blankets around us all the time and then blame circumstances for not achieving what we want to achieve. We see opportunities to make a difference but choose not to act—not take a stand when we know we should.

We don't win back America; we don't win back our lives; we don't win back our families; we don't win back our children; we don't win back our economy, our morality, our American way of life by playing safe and waiting for everything to go perfectly. We can't fix anything by having a Plan B. We do it by fighting for what we know is right! We do it by taking the first step. We do it by making an active choice to be different. We do it by not being a sheep and simply following along because we don't want to upset someone on the other side of a keyboard.

Do something! If you don't like your job, quit it and build a better business, which creates more jobs, which not only fulfills you but also helps the economy and fellow Americans. If you don't like the way the church is being run into a woke culture that is killing religion in our country, then go to seminary and become a warrior for Christ, not a "public figure" pastor.

People come up to me all the time and say things like "I would do what you have done if I had certain assurances." Really? Like, what kind of assurances are you talking about? A guarantee you won't fail and end up bankrupt? Someone to back you with ample financing so you don't have to sweat the big stuff—or the small stuff? People say things like "We need *real* patriots to be in office, but I would *never* try to be elected." They put all the pressure and pass the buck onto someone else because that is the easy thing to do. Where is your courage? How much do you believe in what you claim to believe in? I had an interview with somebody the other day who said that he wanted to come work for the business. I asked what his expectations were, and he asked, "Well, what assurances can you give me?" Wrong answer, and he was immediately eliminated from consideration. He was no longer in the running to be a part of my business, because I'm not selling anybody to come work for me on anything.

Either you believe in what it is that we're trying to do here at *Dear America*, or you don't. Ditto for the Dear America Foundation and Nine Twelve United; believe in them 100 percent, or take a hike. If you don't believe in what we are doing and what we are about down into the deepest reaches of your heart and soul, then get out, because I don't have time for you. If you want to play it safe and have your nest feathered for you, go back home to Mom and Dad and ask them if they have any chores around the house you can do. You want to be part of something great, be prepared to stick your neck out and embrace risk. On a daily basis.

Some of you might believe that sounds harsh, and it is, but that is the way we need to be as Americans. Our battle didn't end when we finally defeated the British after eight years of the Revolutionary War. What are we doing here in 2021 and going forward? What is the point of everything that we're doing? What is the point of doing videos on social media and speaking out on the Internet about the issues facing our country if all you're going to do is whine, gripe, and complain without digging through the kind of research you need in order to be credible and truly informative and inspiring? What good is your voice—and by voice I don't just mean the sound vibrations coming out of your voice box—if you're never going to learn the history of your country? Exactly what kind of change for the good of America do you expect to be if you're never actually going to do anything more than whine and complain on the Internet? Words without actions are less than just words; they are nothing.

Different people are designed and destined to do different things. I understand this. And I understand that it is difficult to decide which path belongs to you. I also understand that it is hard; there's nothing easy about it. I wasn't born doing what I'm doing now, none of which is easy. I'm not the guy who wakes up one day on third base and believes he has hit a triple. What I and hundreds of others like me do is hard. It's not fun having people hate you. It is not fun to lose friends who have been with you your entire life but have since bolted over something as simple as a difference in political views. It isn't fun having death threats and threats of rape against my daughter. None of that is fun. But it is necessary. America is bigger than all of us, and it is worth fighting for!

Let's talk schools. We have to rescue them from the evil that lies within them. The schools are indoctrinating our children, and not in a good way. Not even close. Even the families that are trying to do the best they can at home are losing the battle as soon as their kids are ten, eleven, twelve years old. The schools are determined to indoctrinate them into the liberal mystic belief that the world can be whatever they want it to be. You see, it's not that they lack the potential to achieve whatever they want. They do! The problem is that they are entitled and believe they should be given whatever they want; if anybody dares to tell them otherwise, they are being discriminated against, they are a victim of hate culture, they are a victim of gender identity or hate. On top of that, there's cancel culture and its attempt to reprogram the entire country, starting with our schoolkids. There can be no Plan B. We have to take back our schools. We have to take back the education system.

Teachers need to be vetted to make sure they are not biased pieces of human garbage, because that is what we are largely dealing with right now with rampant political correctness, where wrong is always right. Where there is no set truth. There are "your" truth and "their" truth. We are dealing with a hugely slanted, 90 percent liberal to 10 percent traditional, in terms of how our education leaders are teaching our children within our schools. Our children are no longer our children after the twelfth grade, God forbid college. Those of you reading this book who have kids who have gone off to liberal universities, tell me right now, honestly, were they the same the next time you saw them? A year later? Four years later? The answer is no, they weren't. I don't even have to wait for you to tell me, because I know. I've seen it. I go to those places. I go to those campuses, and I have those debates. Do you? Don't tell me otherwise about what I know to be real. Don't tell me what I know to be true. Because unlike you, what you see on the news, I go to the universities. I have conversations with the kids who hate me because of the values I stand for. Trust me when I say that the indoctrination that is going on with our children is the worst thing that could possibly happen to this society.

If you have a problem with the sexualization of our children, if you have a problem with the attacks against our most innocent because of human trafficking, if you have an issue with pedophilia running rampant within our society, then get up and do something about it. Take the phone away from your children. Heads up, parents, your children have no business having a phone! My kids know, beyond a shadow of a doubt, that they're not going to have a phone until they have a job. And then they're going to have a phone only while they're away at work, so I know they're not dead on the side of the road, and then they're handing it right back to me when they get home, because I will not allow my children to be victims of sexual exploitation. Absolutely not. It will never happen. Those of you who are reading this book and whose child is under the age of twelve and on the Internet, doing whatever he or she wants to do, however he or she wants to do it, you are a part of the problem. Again, please listen to me. *You are a part of the problem. You are letting this happen, sacrificing your child in the process.* How do you feel about that?

You are the reason that there is massive sex trafficking within this country. If you have a problem with our Congress, if you have a problem with our government (you should, because it is by far the worst Congress we have had in the history of our nation), get up and go run for office. "Well, I don't know how to run for office. I'm not a doctor. I'm not a lawyer." Who cares? No one. Go do it. We operate under the illusion that you have to be a lawyer or a doctor or you have to come from money or you have to look a certain way, sound a certain way, to run for office. That is false. That's not the way it was supposed to be. Get up and primary the people who do not deserve to be there.

If you have a problem with your community, if you have a problem with the way crime is running rampant on your streets, run for city council or for mayor. Just go run for some office of influence within your area, and change what needs to be fixed. Do something about it. And for the love of God and everything holy, stop being afraid of what people are going to say to you. Stop being afraid of what someone who lives two thousand miles away from you—someone you will never meet in person—may say about you on the Internet. Who cares? Stop fretting about what they think and feel. Stand up for what you know to be right within a properly functioning society. If you, like me, have a problem with the woke Christianity culture that is taking over the country, wake up and get involved. I said it before, and I will say it again and again: Democratic socialism may take out this country, but I promise you, the cancer that is woke Christianity will kill it first.

If going to seminary, as I mentioned earlier, isn't in the cards for you, at least challenge your pastors to be real pastors. We don't need public figures masquerading as men and women of God while chasing likes and views on Instagram, Twitter, and Facebook. We need real shepherds of the Lord who are standing out there preaching the truth. Jesus never gave a crap about your feelings, and pastors shouldn't care, either. The truth of the Bible deals with the eternal, not the finite that is happening on our streets right now. This life that you crave so desperately is a blip on the radar. You're selfish. I'm selfish. We're all selfish. Every single one of us. And that is the exact opposite of what America is supposed to be. *E pluribus unum*—from many, one. My God, it is time we get back to knowing what America actually stands for.

The primary calling of being an American is caring more about America than about yourself. Caring about your kids' kids more than about yourself. Caring about their children and their children and then their children and their children after that. We just added trillions of dollars to our national debt due to covid-19 relief. Who is going to pay for all of it? We are operating as though we already know that it's over. We're not operating like a nation that is trying to figure out how to last forever; instead, we're looking like a nation hanging on by a thread while trying to figure out what other desperate measures we can put into play before we die. Then our children's children will have to feel the weight of socialism, economic ruin, and, eventually, the takeover of America by another country. I'd bet on China. We are weak, spineless cowards, and we are the direct opposite of what we're supposed to be. That is the truth that no one wants to hear, but it is so very necessary.

We can't allow ourselves to "fade out" because that is exactly what's happening in and to our society right now. We as Americans—*real Americans*; I'm talking about the mentality of being an American and not what your birth certificate says you are—are fading out. It's a disappearing act without the magic. The news isn't getting any better. If we're not careful, it's going to get even worse.

We have an obligation to future generations to burn brighter than ever before. Race, division, political divide— none of it matters. None of it is ever really going to go away regardless of what we do. Some people are always going to think that racism is still rampant within America. No matter what we say, no matter what we do, there are going to be some people who think that the police are bad. Defund them or disband them—that will solve our problems, right? How stupid can we get? No matter what we do, politics will always divide us, but divisiveness is a good thing. Divisiveness of thought leads to further advancement of ideals, and that leads to society's betterment. It's been proven time and time again.

We have to come together and realize that we are Americans. That is the answer. We are not the same, we are actually very different, but we are equal under God. The most important thing about being an American is that America comes first. It is not just America first, it's America *always*! It's not me trying to get my paws on everything I want for myself and then America gets the leftovers. America comes first, and in order to get there, we must invoke the spirit of September 12, 2001, when the spirit of America ruled and everything else was cast aside.

Most of us can still see the images from 9/11 of so many people walking away from the horrific debris of the fallen towers in New York City, their faces and clothing caked in the same light grayish shade of ashes that aptly symbolized what we all had just experienced as a nation. Not since the days of the Japanese attack on Pearl Harbor in December 1941 had we as Americans been so united in our resolve to take the fight to our enemies as we were the day after those terrorist attacks.

As bad as 9/11 was and as iconic as that date has become in American history, we need to invoke September 12, 2001, as the date we should also remember, honor, and emulate as Americans. That was the day we really came together as a nation and petty political differences were shoved aside. Our beginning as a nation might have been 1776, but I can promise you that the spirit of 9/12 is our future. If we do not embrace it, there will be no future for Americans to even have conversations about where we went wrong. We must live every day like it is 9/12. On a day where there was no racial identity, no religious differences, no gender considerations, and no political divide, we showed the world what America was supposed to be. Not that we were a group of people that always got along or always liked one another. But we were Americans, and we were Americans first, and for a time that was how we "identified"—as Americans. And by God, that is what we were going to be about forever—America over Everything.

Twenty years later, how do we fix what's going on? We take a step back in time and live like it's 9/12, which is the only way we can step into the future—with resolve and resiliency. How do we fix the divide within our country? We live like it's 9/12. How do we fix the issues within our school systems? We live like it's 9/12. How do we fix the issues in our own communities? We live like it's 9/12. How do we fix the crime and the issues between the police and the community? We live like it's 9/12. How do we fix societal norms? And how do we fix the degradation of culture within our society? We live like it's 9/12. We owe it to future generations. We owe it to ourselves. We owe it to our children. We owe it to our children's children and then the children's children's children that we will never meet. None of us is guaranteed much time on this earth. How will you choose to live the time that you have?

We fix America by going back to what America actually was supposed to be in the first place. We don't fix America by trying to turn it into something it's not. We don't fix America by believing that a utopian society is possible, because that is a lie. We don't fix America by trying to prove that our thought processes are superior to all others'. No. We fix America by realizing that, as Americans, we are all different—we are never going to see eye to eye on everything. But we *can* see eye to eye on one thing, and that's the fact that we are Americans.

If you've made it through this book, one of two things has happened. Either you hate me, or you are me. Either you think I'm crazy, or you think like I think and you feel like I feel. If you made it through this book, you know that I'm right. If you've made it through this book, it's time to get up and time to do something.

Are you still here?

Good.

We have a lot of work to do, and it's time we got started.

ACKNOWLEDGMENTS

First and foremost, I want to thank God for giving me the grace I have never and will never deserve. I will never understand the life you have given me, but I am truly grateful every single day.

To my beautiful wife, Ellisa, thank you for loving me. If people only knew the *real* me like you do, I am not sure anyone would still be here. However, you choose me every single day, and I am so thankful for that. You are the rock that holds our family together. To my beautiful children, Gage, Gunnar, and AnnaGrace, I hope you know how much you are loved. Most of all, I hope you learn that if I can achieve something, you can achieve *anything*! You and your mom are the people I strive to make the most proud of me.

To my business partner, Jason, thank you for believing in me when no one else did. Thank you for working for nothing when I couldn't afford to pay you a single cent. I wouldn't be here today without your willingness to believe. I thank you for that.

To my friends Justin, Gary, Bryson, Brandi, Todd, Jake, Noah, and everyone else it would take too long to write, thank you for believing in me. Thank you for supporting this crazy idea I had so many years ago. Thank you for being my family. Thank you for literally everything.

Finally, thank you, the reader, viewer, listener, subscriber, and fellow patriots, for trusting me. Thank you for sticking with me for over four years! Thank you for trusting me to say what you want to be heard. Thank you for allowing me the privilege to live the life I live. Thank you for being Americans. Lastly, thank you for allowing me into your lives daily! It is truly a gift I will never take for granted.

ABOUT THE AUTHOR

GRAHAM ALLEN is a former army staff sergeant and served twelve years in combat, including two tours during Operation Iraqi Freedom. Today, he is the host of the podcast *Dear America*, and he was named one of the *Huffington Post*'s "22 veterans to watch in 2017." In 2020, he released the book *America 3:16* to critical acclaim.